CW01237963

BRANCH LINES AROUND WROXHAM

Richard Adderson and Graham Kenworthy

MP *Middleton Press*

Front cover: In a classic East Anglian branch line scene of the era, class J17 0-6-0 no.65534 waits alongside Reepham signal box with a goods train in April 1952. The driver and fireman smile down from the cab at the photographer, who was a signalman on the line, and as such would know exactly how much time he had to compose his picture. (E.Tuddenham/P.J.A.Bower/M&GN Circle)

Back cover upper: No.08250 creeps cautiously across the road at Belaugh Green level crossing (see also picture 47) on the afternoon of 29th September 1979. It is on its way to Lenwade with one of the enthusiasts' specials which occasionally ventured on to this little known railway byway. (R.J.Adderson)

Back cover lower: Almost exactly 32 years later, on 25th September 2011, the crossing is still in use, even though the trains are considerably smaller. The Ravenglass and Eskdale Railway's **Northern Rock** *is seen at the same location, while a making a guest appearance on the occasion of a Bure Valley Railway Gala. (R.J.Adderson)*

Published September 2012

ISBN 978 1 908174 31 4

© Middleton Press, 2012

Design Deborah Esher

Published by
    Middleton Press
    Easebourne Lane
    Midhurst
    West Sussex
    GU29 9AZ
Tel: 01730 813169
Fax: 01730 812601
Email: info@middletonpress.co.uk
www.middletonpress.co.uk

Printed in the United Kingdom by Henry Ling Limited, at the Dorset Press, Dorchester, DT1 1HD

CONTENTS

1. Norwich Thorpe to North Walsham   1-46
2. Wroxham to County School   47-120

INDEX

69	Aylsham	106	Foulsham	13	Salhouse
58	Buxton Lamas	27	Hoveton & Wroxham	5	Whitlingham Junction
81	Cawston	39	North Walsham	34	Worstead
48	Coltishall	1	Norwich Thorpe	18	Wroxham
117	County School	88	Reepham		

ACKNOWLEDGEMENTS

In addition to those individuals acknowledged in the photographic credits, we are most grateful to G.Hawkins, A.Rush, M.Storey-Smith, and A.Whittaker.

Readers of this book may be interested in the following society:

Great Eastern Railway Society,
Peter Walker, Membership Secretary, 24 Bacons Drive,
Cuffley, Herts. EN6 4DU

Railways of the area in the 1954 showing pre-grouping ownerships.
Other maps in this volume are to a scale of 25 ins to 1 mile, unless otherwise stated.

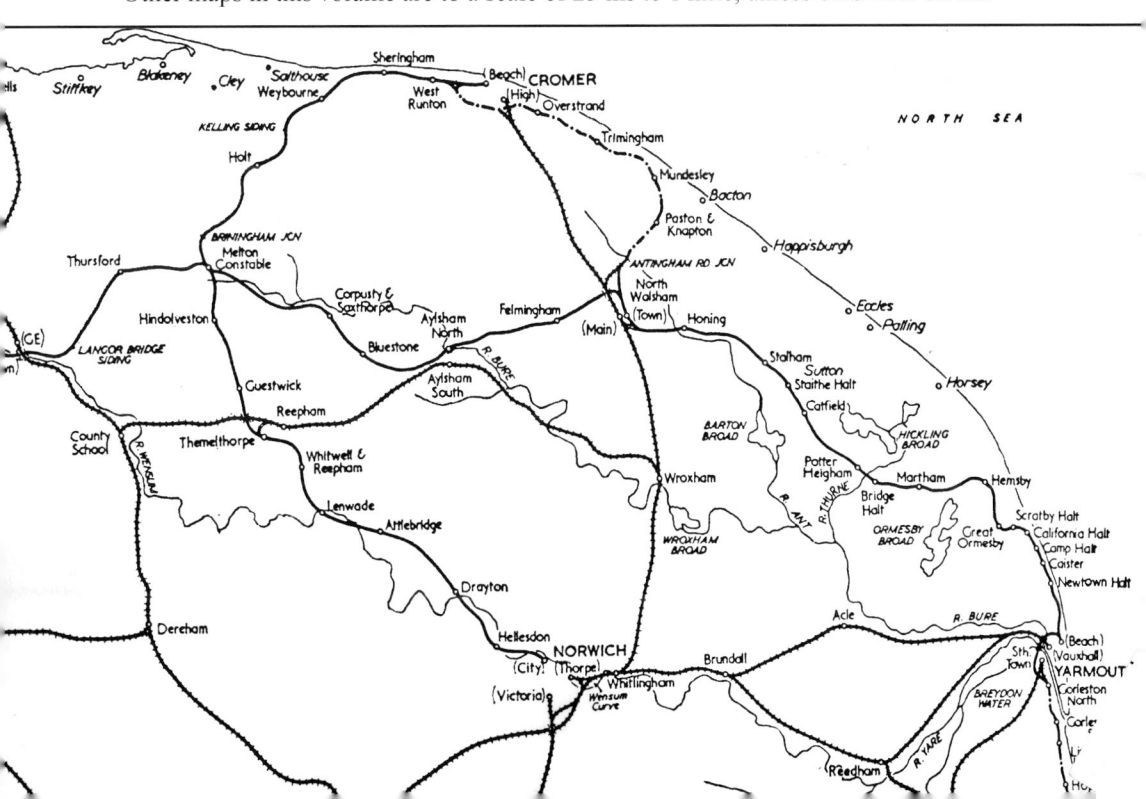

GEOGRAPHICAL SETTING

Whitlingham Junction to North Walsham

From the junction with the line to Yarmouth and Lowestoft, the route is faced with a steep climb out of the Yare Valley towards a summit around 100 feet higher just before Salhouse. There follows a slightly shallower descent into the Bure Valley at Wroxham. Apart from a slight dip near Worstead, the branch continues to climb towards North Walsham which is about 130 feet above its origin at Whitlingham. The northern end of what has become known as the *Bittern Line* from North Walsham to Cromer and Sheringham was covered in our earlier volume *Branch Lines Around Cromer*.

Wroxham to County School

Although the River Bure takes a somewhat meandering course north west from Wroxham towards Aylsham, the line is never far away and is, therefore, free of steep gradients. Beyond Aylsham the route leaves the Bure Valley and climbs to a generally higher level before falling to the junction near County School, located in a third river valley, that of the Wensum.

Both routes were constructed predominantly on clay.

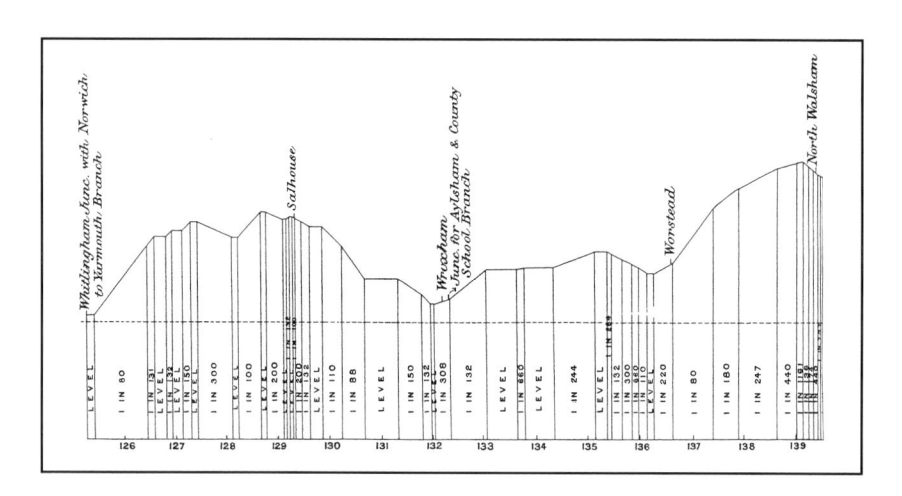

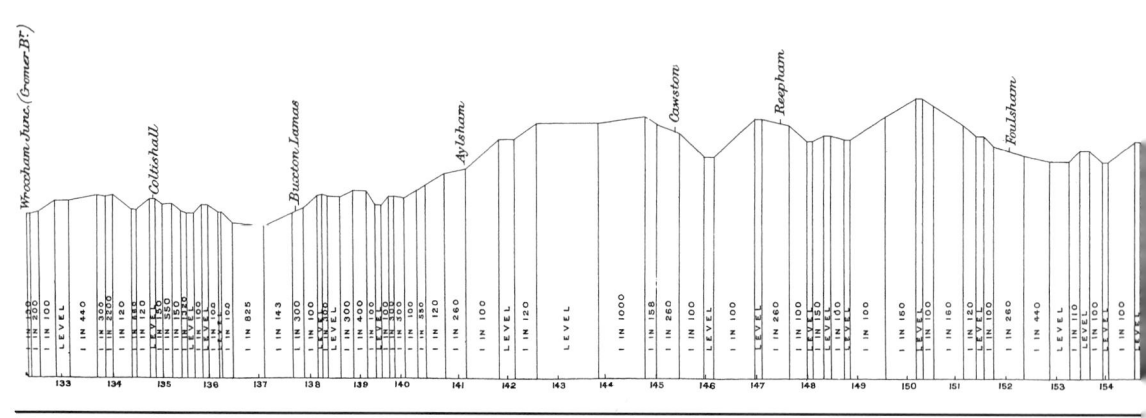

HISTORICAL BACKGROUND

Whitlingham Junction to North Walsham

The first East Norfolk Railway Act, for the line from Whitlingham Junction, on the eastern outskirts of Norwich, to North Walsham, had been passed in 1864, with construction work starting the following year. Various complications led to an early halt in proceedings, with a resumption of work being delayed until 1870. An Act for an extension of time (and for further authority for a line from North Walsham to Cromer) was required in 1872. The line, which was single, eventually opened in sections, as far as North Walsham on 20th October 1874, on to Gunton on 29th July 1876, and to Cromer on 26th March 1877. The East Norfolk Railway Company was absorbed into the Great Eastern Railway in 1881.

Increased demand for services led to the doubling of the line in two sections (Whitlingham to Wroxham and Wroxham to North Walsham) between 1896 and 1901.

The Great Eastern Railway passed into the ownership of the London & North Eastern Railway on 1st January 1923, and the lines became part of the Eastern Region of British Railways upon nationalisation on 1st January 1948.

Following closure of other lines in the area in the 1950s and a general contraction in the mid-1960s following the Beeching Report, the section from Wroxham to North Walsham was singled on 15th January 1967.

However, the route survived, serving Cromer and Sheringham on the north coast, and providing a useful commuter and holiday service for the remainder of the 20th century and into the 21st. Privatisation meant operation by Anglia Railways from 5th January 1997 and latterly under the Greater Anglia franchise.

Wroxham to County School

Conscious of the potential threat of a west to east line across Norfolk from the Kings Lynn direction, the East Norfolk Company, no doubt in conjunction with the Great Eastern Railway, promoted a line westwards in two stages. The first East Norfolk Act in 1876 authorised the route from Wroxham to Aylsham while the second, in 1879, covered the extension to Broom Green Junction, between North Elmham and Ryburgh on the Wymondham to Wells line. The single line branch opened in no less than five separate sections as follows:-

Wroxham to Buxton Lamas	8th July 1879
Buxton Lamas to Aylsham	1st January 1880
Aylsham to Cawston	1st September 1880
Cawston to Reepham	2nd May 1881
Reepham to Broom Green Junction	1st May 1882

However, Broom Green Junction was eliminated when County School station opened on 1st March 1884 and the single line extended south to that station.

Grouping in 1923 and Nationalisation in 1948 followed the same pattern as the North Walsham line, but the latter event resulted in the withdrawal of passenger services on 15th September 1952. The freight only line between Foulsham and Reepham was closed on 7th February 1955 with Foulsham served from the County School end and Reepham from the Wroxham end. In January 1957 Wroxham to Reepham became a Light Railway with an order extending the Light Railway westwards to Themelthorpe following in March 1960. This later order was necessary to link up with the former M&GN route to Norwich.

This part of the line survived carrying several different categories of freight traffic, and occasional passenger specials, for 24 years until June 1983. Details of these services are included in the main body of the book.

In 1990, with the backing of Broadland District Council, the privately owned 15-inch gauge Bure Valley Railway was opened sharing the former trackbed between Wroxham and Aylsham with a public footpath. It celebrated its 21st birthday in July 2011, by which time it had developed into a major tourist attraction, recording over 120,000 passenger journeys in each of the years 2009-2011.

PASSENGER SERVICES

Norwich Thorpe to North Walsham

The timetable for February 1875, before the northward extension from North Walsham was opened, showed six weekday services.

The subsequent extension helped in developing Cromer as a fashionable resort and by the Winter timetable of 1912/13 there were nine trains serving the line, two of which were through restaurant car expresses from Liverpool Street, calling only at Wroxham and North Walsham.

By 1938, with the public's increased appetite for travel, the number had increased to around thirteen, including similar through services from London.

In 1970, there were still thirteen trains listed, although the through services from the capital had disappeared some years previously; a small number of the trains did not call at the smaller stations at Salhouse and Worstead.

By 2012, a revival in local services had seen the provision of seventeen trains, still with a number not serving Salhouse and Worstead.

Wroxham to County School

Needless to say that, with the line opening in such a piecemeal fashion, early services changed quite frequently to serve the newly opened sections. When the first service commenced to Buxton Lamas, it took the form of a shuttle service from Wroxham. However, when the route was extended to Aylsham, the Norfolk Chronicle suggested that through trains (from Norwich) were introduced.

With the opening of County School station in 1884 at the western end of the line, there were a significant number of alterations listed in the same newspaper, but there were no references to any through services. The timetable for November of that year indicated seven weekday services throughout calling at all stations, with two trains running to Dereham and one terminating at Foulsham; a slightly different pattern applied on Saturdays.

In March 1920, by which time the line from Whitlingham Junction to Wroxham had long since been doubled, all six weekday services originated at Norwich Thorpe. Five of these ran through to Dereham, with just the first of the day terminating at County School.

Around 1930 the introduction of a number of steam railmotors to the Norwich area led to a slight increase in the number of services. In the 1938 timetable there were seven services in total along the line of which five ran through from Norwich Thorpe to Dereham; two were provided by these vehicles, and a further one provided a return service to Aylsham.

The Summer 1950 timetable showed six trains serving all stations and terminating at Dereham; all but two of these originated at Norwich.

The Bure Valley Railway ran trains on 213 days of the year in 1991, a figure that had increased to 261 days in 2012. The 2012 timetable showed trains running every day from April to October, and at weekends and on other occasions during the remaining months (except for January). At peak times, there were six daily round trips from Aylsham.

September 1885

Railway timetable, September 1952.

Table 55 NORWICH (Thorpe), WROXHAM, NORTH WALSHAM, MUNDESLEY-ON-SEA, CROMER, and SHERINGHAM

Table 57 NORWICH (Thorpe), WROXHAM, AYLSHAM (South), COUNTY SCHOOL, and DEREHAM

1. Norwich Thorpe to North Walsham
NORWICH THORPE

1.   Continuing development of the railway routes into the city led the Great Eastern Railway to build a brand new terminus, which was opened in 1886, close to the site of the earlier station which dated back to 1844. This imposing new station was a source of great civic pride, and externally the building changed little over the years. The cars parked in the forecourt suggest this view dates from around 1959, when the all day parking fee was one shilling. (NRS Archive)

2.   Class B12 4-6-0 no. 61568 stands in platform 3 on 12th May 1953, ready to leave for Cromer and Sheringham at 2.52 pm. The train had set out as the 12.30 pm from Liverpool Street, and at the time it was one of no fewer than six daily through trains between London and Cromer, and sometimes beyond, which reversed at Norwich. (P.J Kelley)

3. Carrow Road bridge, spanning the station approaches, was a favourite location for trainspotters and photographers alike, providing good views of the railway operations in both directions. With the station in the distance, class B1 4-6-0 no. 61043 passes a fine array of signals as it leaves with a five coach train bound for the Cromer line on 5th October 1952. The engine was a familiar sight here, being allocated to Norwich shed for nearly all of its existence. (R.Harrison)

4. Now we cross the bridge to see class A5 4-6-2T no. 69824 nearing the end of its journey with a train from the East Norfolk line on a sunny 15th March 1953, with the lines to Ely and Ipswich diverging to the right. The engine was one of a handful of these former Great Central Railway locomotives which could be found in the area during the early 1950s. (R.Harrison)

WHITLINGHAM JUNCTION

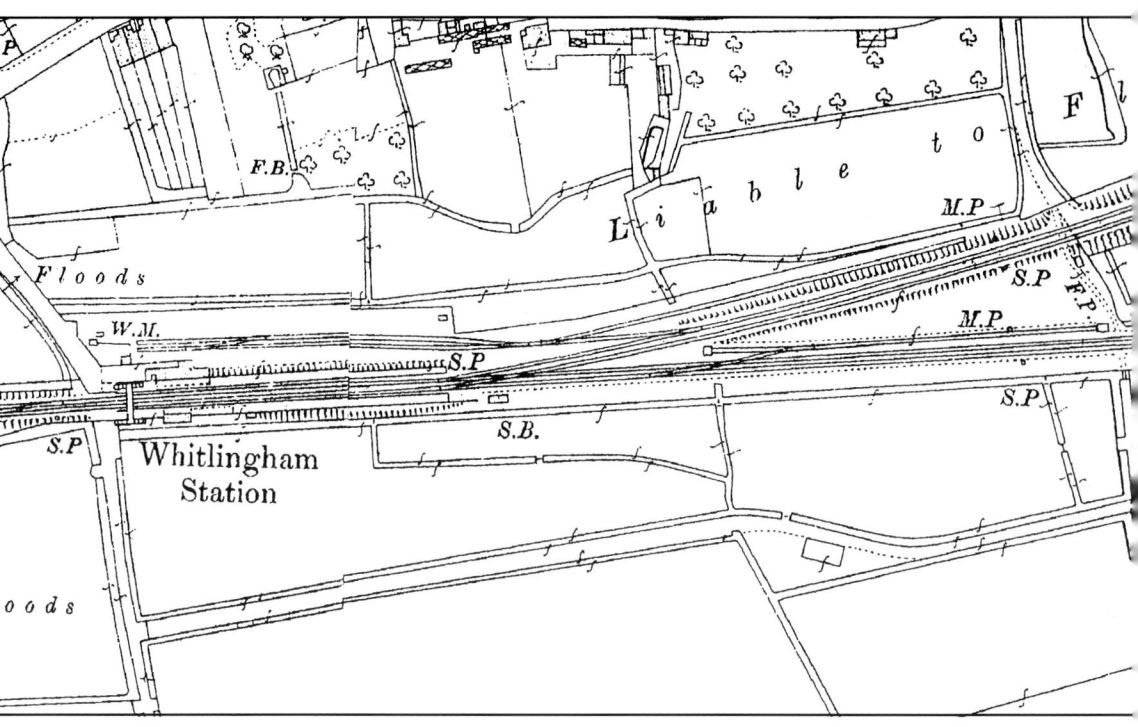

1. The station was opened as an interchange facility when the route we are following towards North Walsham was opened in 1874. This 1914 plan shows the layout as it existed following the provision of a goods yard in 1902. Closure took place in 1955 despite many local protests.

5. Whilst the earlier line to Brundall followed the river valley and was easily graded, the East Norfolk line faced a stiff climb away from the valley. We are looking westwards down the bank towards the station on 27th September 1911, with the marshy nature of the land very much in evidence, and the River Yare in the distance. (GERS/Windwood coll.)

6. Some three years later, Mr Lawrence, the Whitlingham station master, poses with a group of Red Cross Voluntary nurses, who were using a coach parked in the goods yard as a training school. He must have been the envy of his colleagues as they dealt with their mundane daily consignments of coal and cattle! (Thorpe History Group coll.)

7. The photographer is looking eastwards from the footbridge as class B17 4-6-0 no. 61656 *Leeds United* runs through the station with a train from the Cromer line on a sunny day in the early 1950s. A fenced off portion of platform marks the site of a small waiting shelter which had been demolished as the result of subsidence problems. (I.C.Allen/Transport Treasury)

8.   Around the same time, a class B1 4-6-0 heads a down train towards the deserted platforms. Trains on each of the various routes from Norwich to the coast carried an individual headcode, and the disc on the buffer beam indicates that this one will be taking the Cromer line at the junction, while the modern coaches suggest that it is one of the through trains from London. The canopy on the building is beginning to show signs of age, and it was removed before the station closed on 19th September 1955. (R.J.Adderson coll.)

➔ 9. A class B12 4-6-0, no. 61568, is working hard as it attacks the sharp 1 in 80 gradient out of the station with a stopping train for the Cromer line, again during the early 1950s. (I.C.Allen/Transport Treasury)

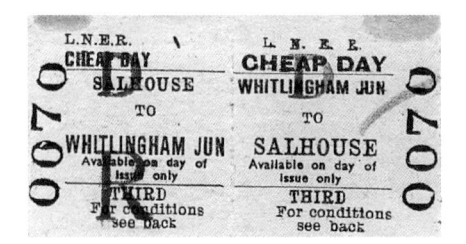

➔ 10. A Brush type 4 diesel waits at the signals by the junction in May 1968, with a train of container flats bound for North Walsham. It will return with the first of many trainloads of containers manufactured in the town. At this time, the goods yard was in regular use for cement traffic. (G.H.Smith)

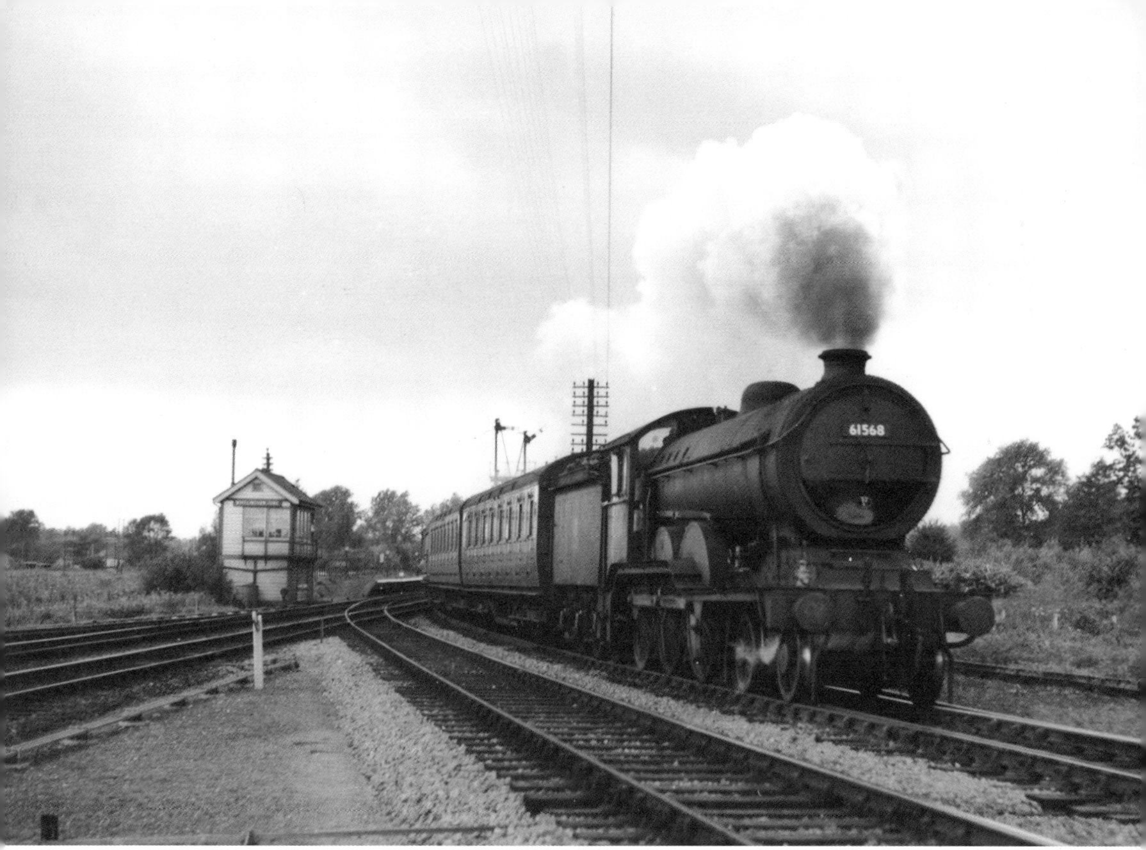
61568

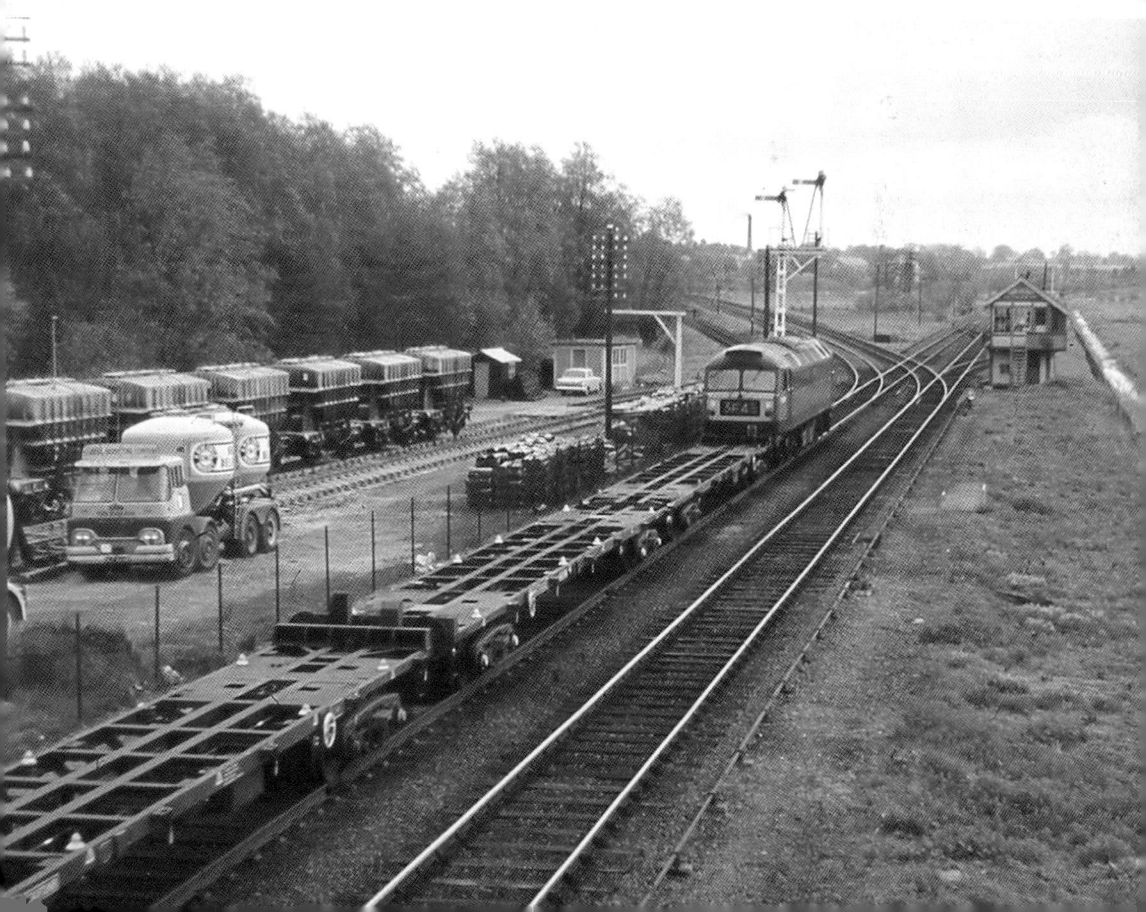

11.   Staying on the footbridge, which survived to provide pedestrian access to the marshes and riverside, we see a train from the East Norfolk line negotiating the junction on 3rd August 1985. With the semaphore signals and signal box, it is still very much of a traditional scene, even though there is no longer any trace of the platforms. In the distance, another train stands at the outer home signal, waiting for the line to Brundall to become clear - at the time this was a very busy stretch of railway on Summer Saturdays. (R.J.Adderson)

12.   The junction semaphore signals were a victim of the Norwich resignalling scheme during the summer of 1986, and the signal box was demolished in June 2000, following the introduction of a new signalling system on what had become known as the "Bittern Line". Following these changes, the view from the footbridge is very different on 1st September 2011, as no.37601 leads a test train off the branch towards Norwich. (R.J.Adderson)

SALHOUSE

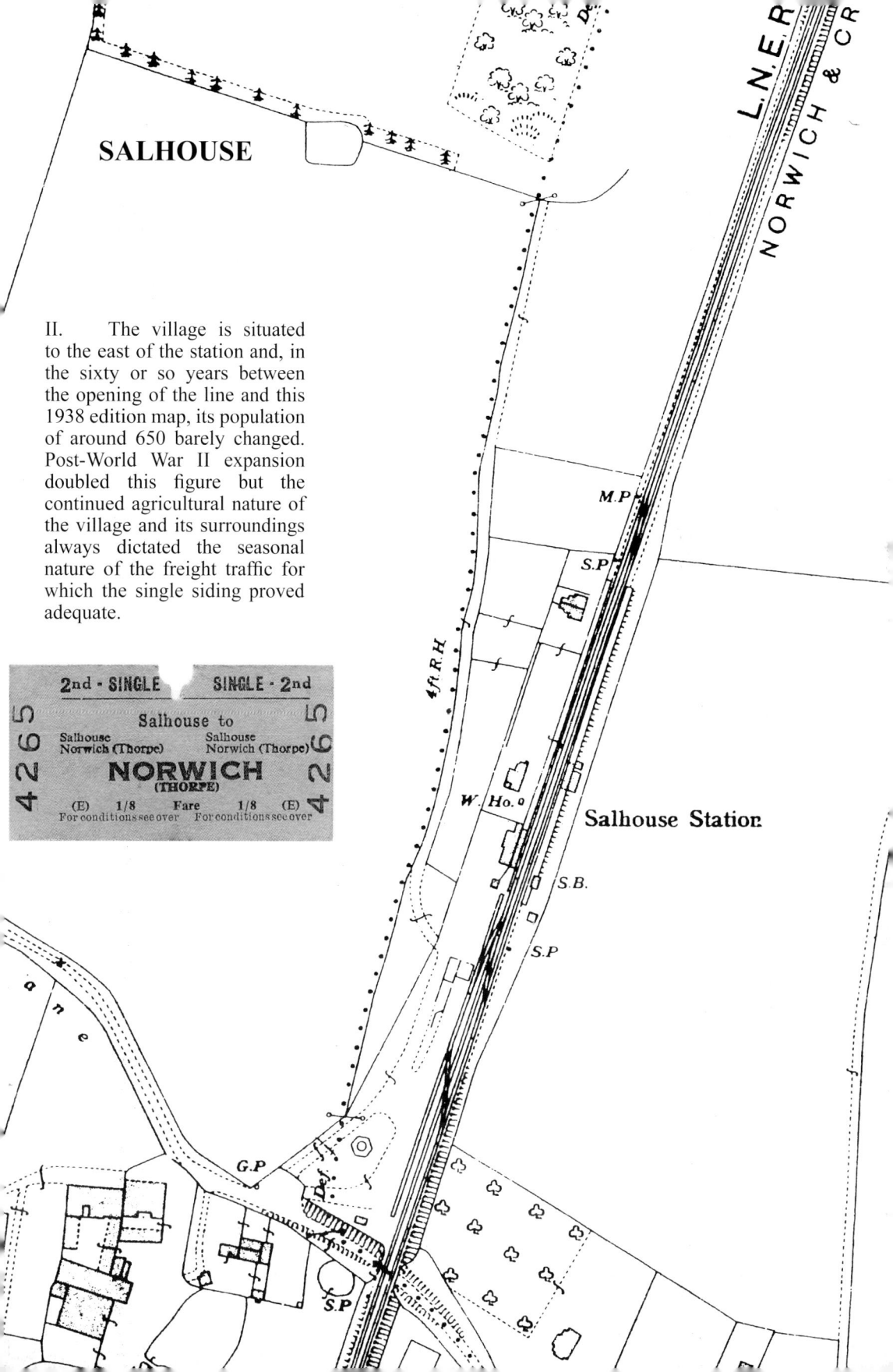

II. The village is situated to the east of the station and, in the sixty or so years between the opening of the line and this 1938 edition map, its population of around 650 barely changed. Post-World War II expansion doubled this figure but the continued agricultural nature of the village and its surroundings always dictated the seasonal nature of the freight traffic for which the single siding proved adequate.

13.	The signal box dominates the view southwards from the up platform in July 1966, but it is a scene which will not last much longer. Following the withdrawal of goods facilities some three months earlier, the single siding is overgrown and will soon be lifted, while the box was closed on 11th July 1966 and the empty shell demolished early in 1968.
(Railway Record of the British Isles/G.L.Pring)

14.	Moving a little further along the platform on the same day, we can see that the wooden building on the down side is still in use, and appears to be well maintained. The station name appears in quick succession on the blue enamel running in board, the cast iron seat back nameplate, and the totem sign, leaving passengers in no doubt as to their whereabouts.
(Railway Record of the British Isles/G.L.Pring)

15.	A class 31 diesel heads a condensate train through the station on a sunny day in January 1970. This traffic flow, carrying waste materials to Harwich from the North Sea gas terminal at Bacton, began in the late 1960s and was still providing a useful source of revenue in 2012. At this time the train originated at Coltishall, as the purpose built sidings at North Walsham were not yet complete. (G.H.Smith)

G. E. R.

Salhouse

16. The station became an unstaffed halt from 2nd January 1967, but the buildings remained in place for some years, albeit locked out of use. Superficially, little has changed on 1st August 1974, as the 10.04 am from Liverpool Street to Sheringham departs. Running only on Summer Saturdays, this train was the final through working between London and the branch, other than a short lived and inconveniently timed train provided as a franchise requirement on privatisation. It ran for the last time in 1975. (R.J.Adderson)

17. Although the main offices had long been demolished and replaced by a "bus shelter", the building on the down platform was still standing in 2012, with the canopy offering some degree of shelter to waiting passengers. No. 57003 heads north with a Rail Head Treatment Train (RHTT) on 4th November 2011. These seasonal workings help to keep train services running at times when falling leaves are liable to make track conditions difficult. (R.J.Adderson)

WROXHAM

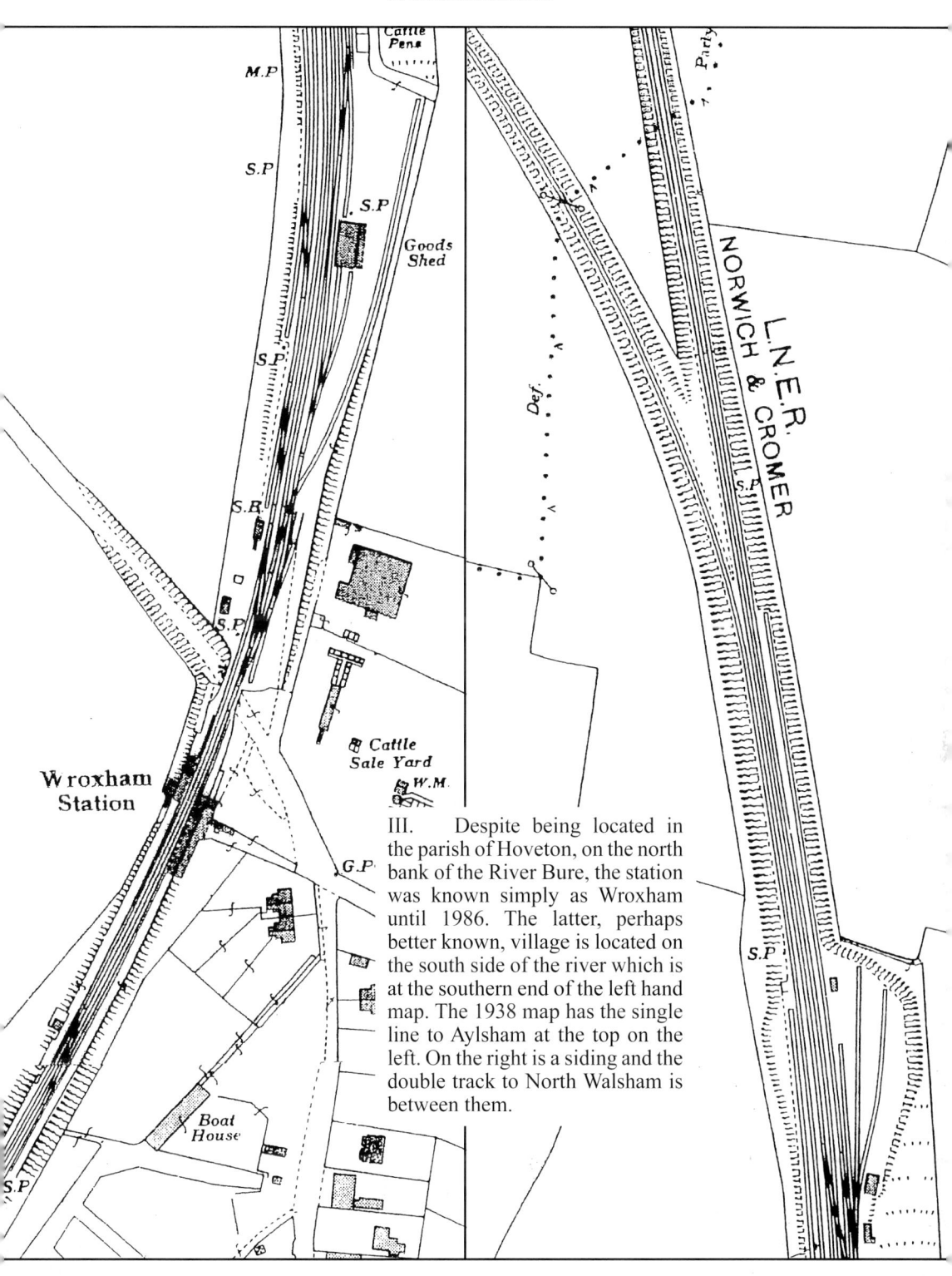

Cattle Pens
M.P
S.P
S.P
Goods Shed
S.P
L.N.E.R. NORWICH & CROMER
S.R
Def.
S.P
S.P
Wroxham Station
Cattle Sale Yard
W.M.
G.P
S.P
Boat House
S.P

III. Despite being located in the parish of Hoveton, on the north bank of the River Bure, the station was known simply as Wroxham until 1986. The latter, perhaps better known, village is located on the south side of the river which is at the southern end of the left hand map. The 1938 map has the single line to Aylsham at the top on the left. On the right is a siding and the double track to North Walsham is between them.

18.   We are standing at the northern end of the goods yard on 27th September 1911, and the raw earth to the right suggests that the sidings had recently been extended. The double track line towards North Walsham goes straight ahead into the distance, while the Aylsham branch curves away in the cutting immediately to the left of the furthest signal. The short lived Yard signal box, abolished by 1929, is dwarfed by the tall signal post controlling traffic from the branch. (GERS/Windwood coll.)

→ 19. We are now looking northwards from the Station signal box, again on 27th September 1911. Goods are being transferred between road and rail transport in the yard to the right, and the cattle pens beyond the goods shed cater for another important traffic flow in the rural economy. The wooden coaling platform to the left was provided for locomotives working the County School branch, but is noticeably devoid of fuel on this occasion. (GERS/Windwood coll.)

→   20. A few years later, horse drawn traffic is very much in evidence as a group of people stand in front of the wooden station building, watching the photographer with varying degrees of self-consciousness. The smaller building on the up platform is a former signal box, and in front of it, we can see that W H Smith have arrived on the scene. This company was still running a bookstall from the station forecourt, although in a different position, during the late 1960s. (Philip Standley coll.)

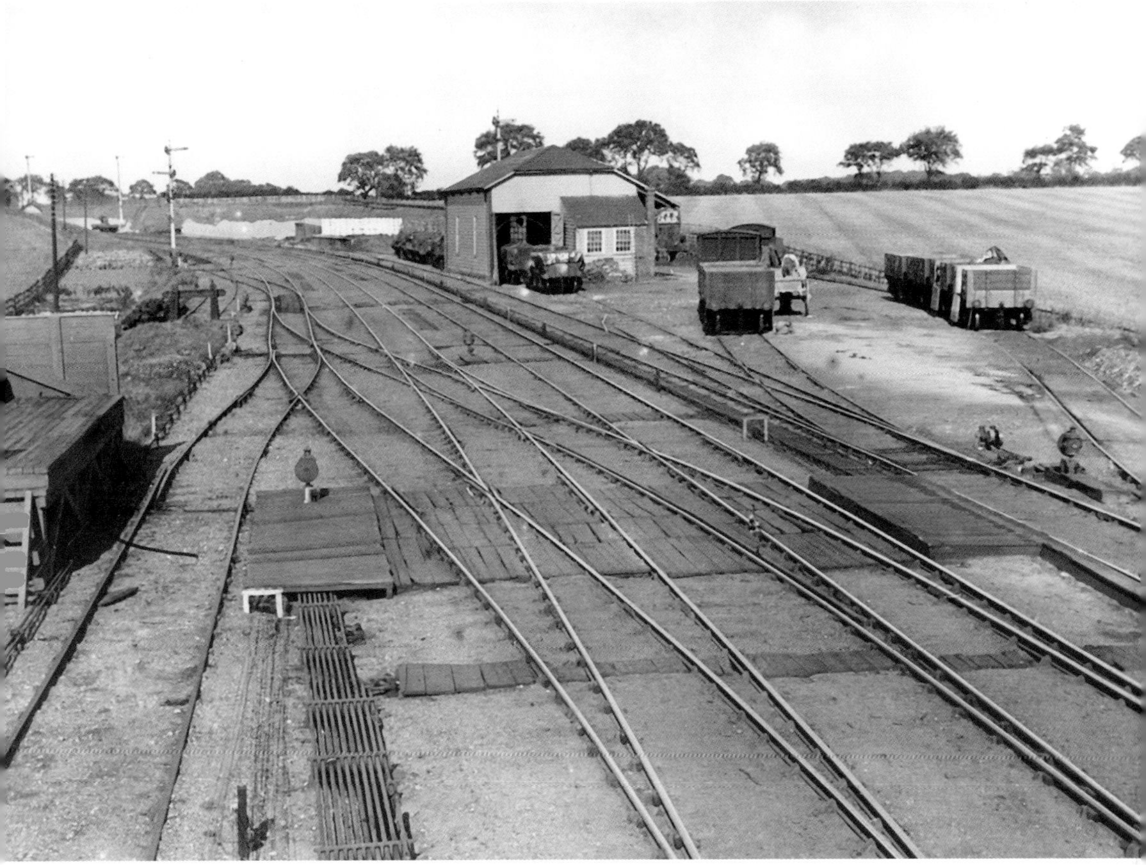

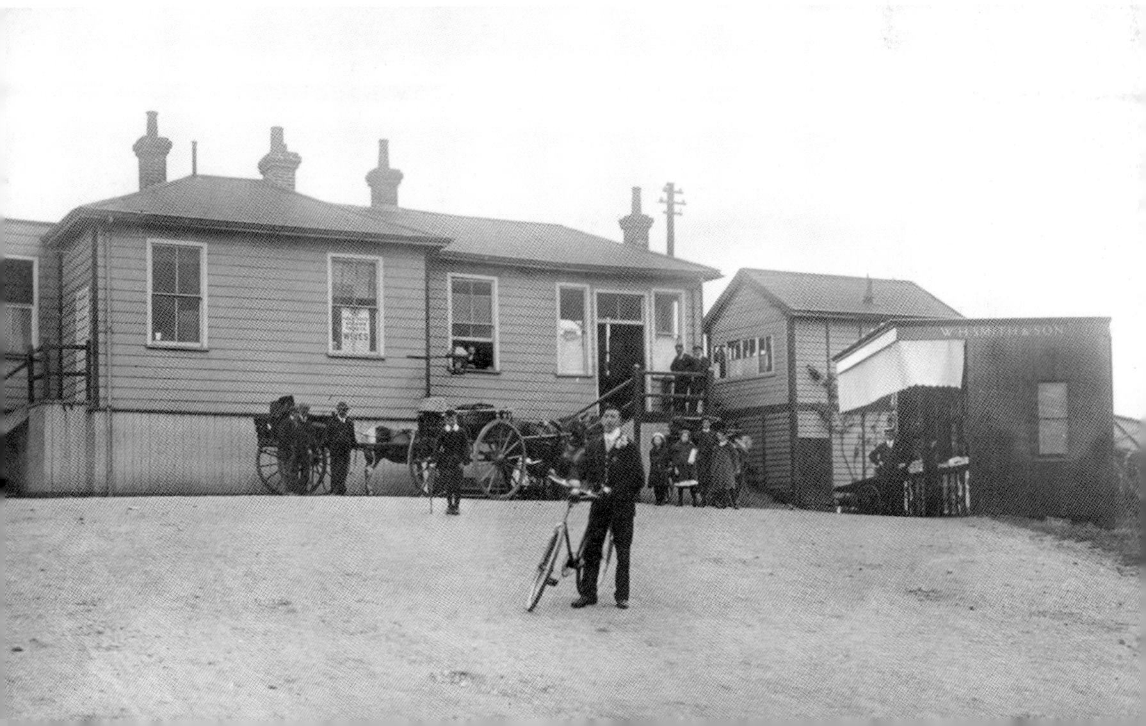
WIVES
W H SMITH & SON

21.   During the 1920s and 1930s, the LNER used a number of steam railcars on certain branch line and local workings. These machines were never common in East Anglia, but a few came to Norfolk, and their diagrams included some trains on the Wroxham to County School line. This example has just crossed the river bridge to the south of the station on one such service which had originated at Norwich. (G.L.Kenworthy coll.)

➔ 22. Here we have a busy scene, looking northwards from the end of the up platform on 28th May 1949, with class D16/3 4-4-0 no. 62581 running into the station, past a water crane. The tracks fanned out to cover a wide area north of the road bridge, and the variety of signals reflects the resultant complex trackwork. At ground level, the shunt signals are for the crossovers and yard access, while the three arms on the post to the left control, from left to right, and in increasing order of importance, a siding, the Aylsham line and the main line towards Worstead and beyond. Completing the activity, another locomotive lurks in the goods yard to the right. (R.E.Vincent/Transport Treasury)

➔ 23. The station was built on a long thin site, with two platforms atop an embankment. The buildings were at the north end, and although there had been various waiting shelters on the up platform over the years, these had been demolished by the time this picture was taken in the mid 1950s. A water tower is the only feature at the otherwise bare southern end of the platforms. (Lens of Sutton coll.)

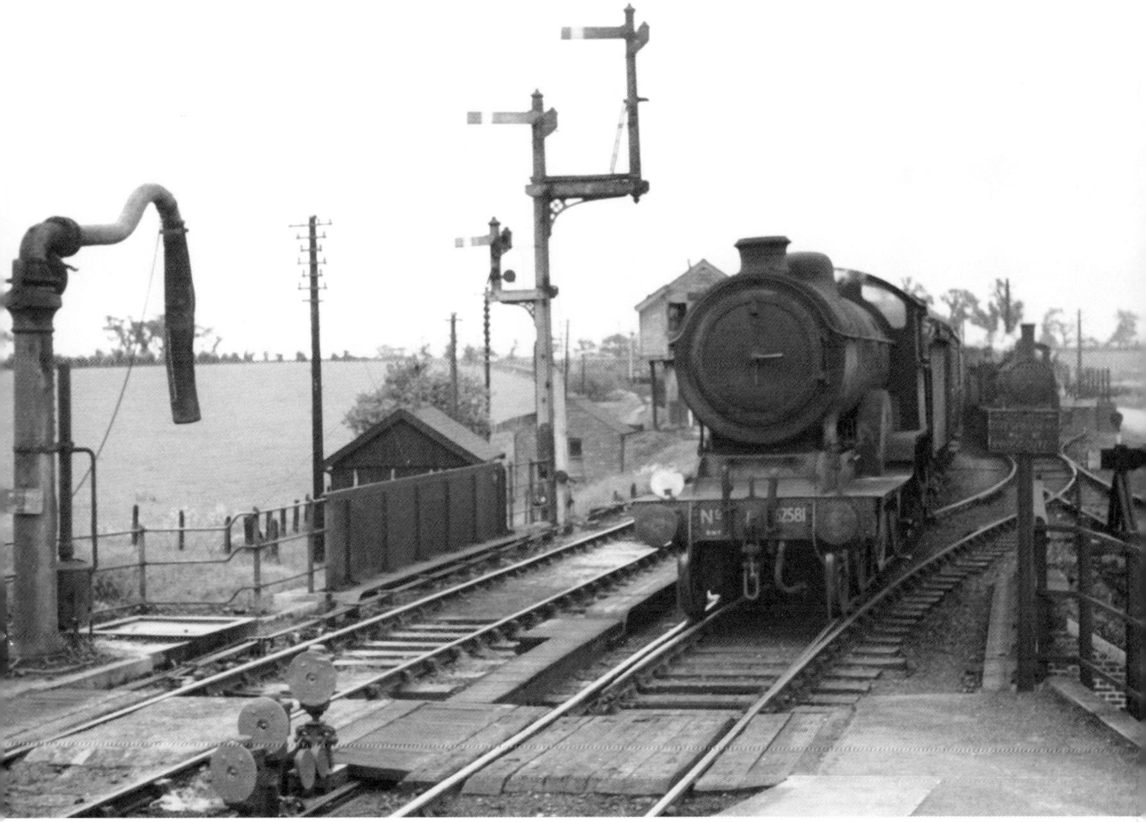

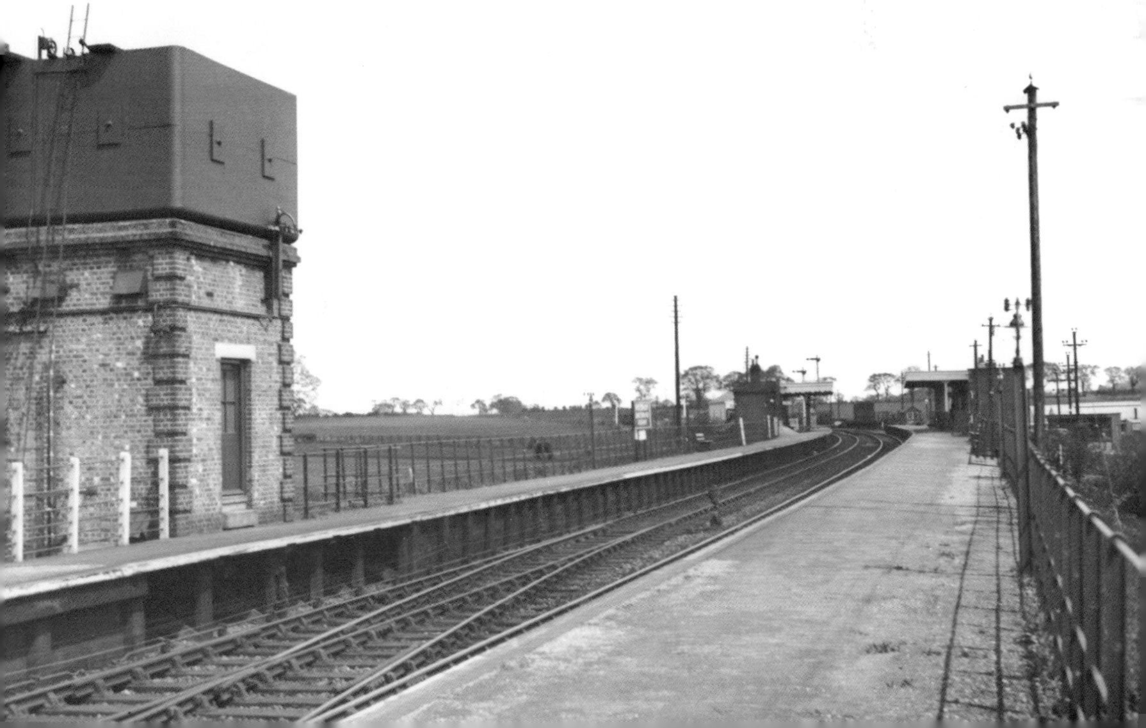

24. The wooden buildings shown in picture 20 were replaced in the mid 1930s by these rather functional brick built structures. A sand train from Coltishall is approaching, hauled by a pair of class 15 diesel locomotives, on 14th August 1967. The scene as depicted here had changed only in detail by 2012. (Railway Record of the British Isles/G.L.Pring)

➜ 25. The signal indicates that this goods train is taking the branch to Aylsham. It is April 1969, and nobody could have imagined that, in just over twenty one years time, the area to the left of the signal box would be occupied by the terminal station of a 15" gauge railway. The little brick hut remained in place in 2012, together with the signal box, which had been moved to a slightly different position following purchase for preservation by a group of enthusiasts. (G.H.Smith)

➜ 26. The driver leans from his cab to hand the single line token to the signalman as a train for Norwich approaches the station on 11th July 1969. Traditional scenes such as this would disappear in 2000 with the introduction of a new signalling system on the branch, controlled from Trowse Swing Bridge in Norwich.
(Railway Record of the British Isles/G.L.Pring)

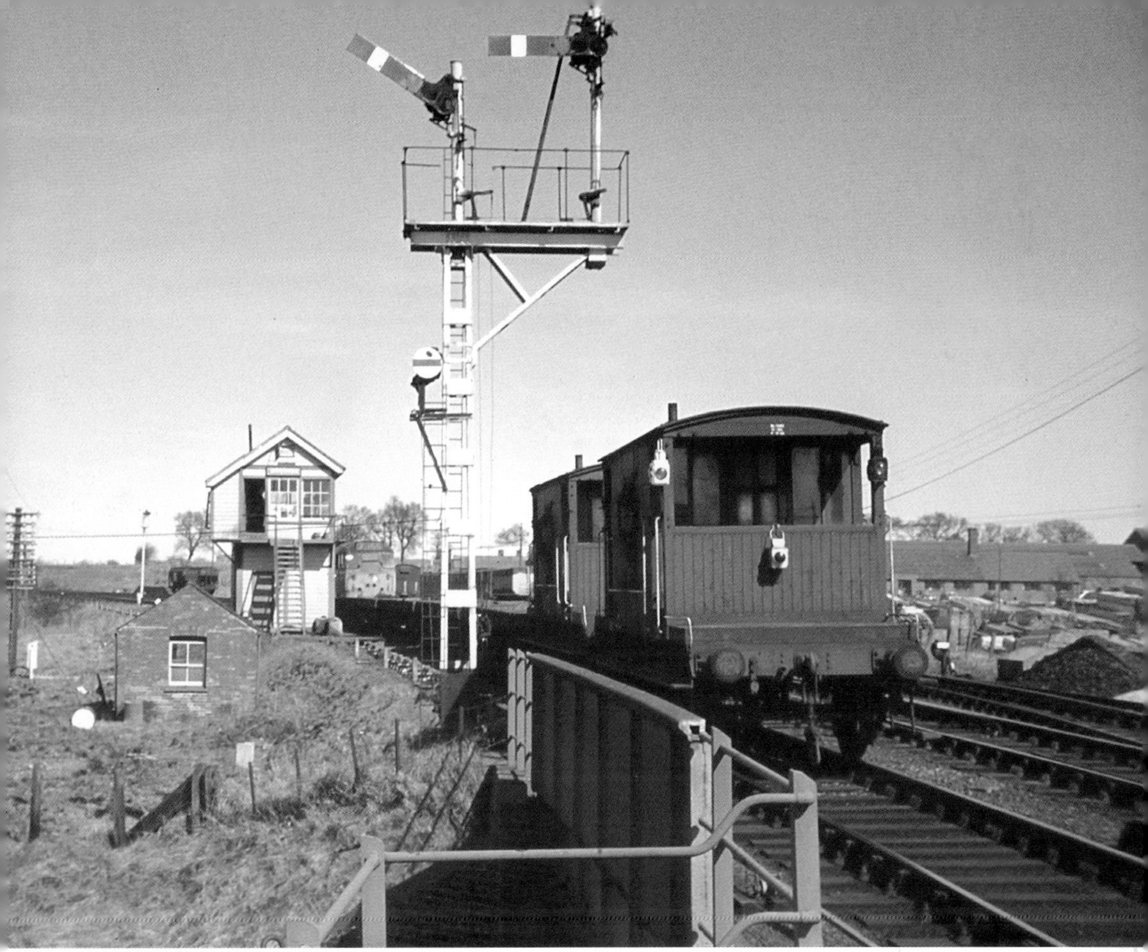

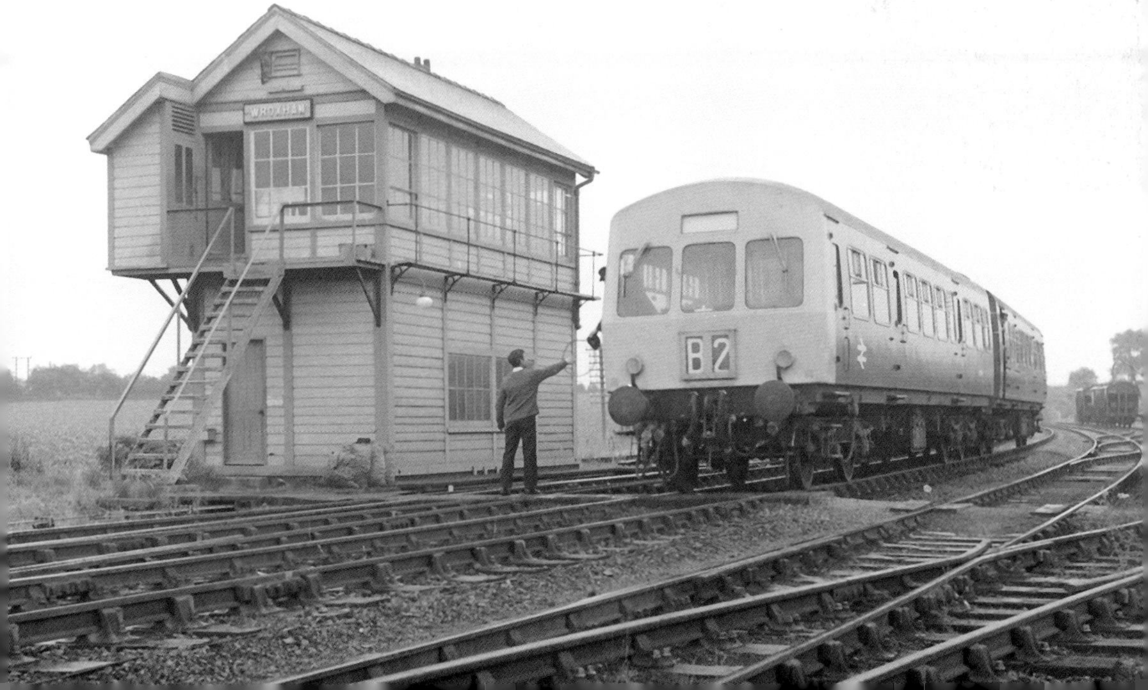

WROXHAM
B2

HOVETON & WROXHAM

27. The goods yard continued to handle irregular trainloads of outward grain traffic into the 1990s, ceasing only when British Rail closed down their Speedlink freight operation in 1991. This was the scene on 14th November 1988, with a lorry unloading grain into the waiting railway wagon. (J.R.Sides)

28. Work on the construction of the Bure Valley station was well underway on 25th February 1990. The exterior structure, canopy, and platform edging are seemingly complete, but there is a lot of work to be done before the narrow gauge rails can be laid. We are looking southwards, and the main line signal box is to the left of the picture. (R.J.Adderson)

29. With the rusting tracks of the abandoned goods yard to the left, a class 66 approaches the station with the North Walsham to Harwich condensate train on 5th May 1999. Following privatisation of the railway network, this traffic was worked by EWS, before GB Railfreight won the contract during 2005. The photographer has opted for an elevated viewpoint, allowing a view of the Bure Valley Railway station beyond the train. (D.C.Pearce)

30. The town is renowned as an important centre in the Broads, but rail passengers get no more than a hint of this as their train rumbles across the bridge over the River Bure. However, the boatyards and waterways are not far away, as we see from this picture of no. 66178 nearing the station with a special train on 19th September 2009. (M. Page)

→ 31. Bure Valley Railway ZB class 2-6-2 no. 6 *Blickling Hall* has arrived with a passenger train, and will shortly be uncoupled and run forward on to the turntable. There are two other locomotives in evidence, and the level of activity confirms that this picture was taken on the occasion of one of the Railway's Gala Days, 13th September 2008. The standard gauge lines are in the foreground. (M.Page)

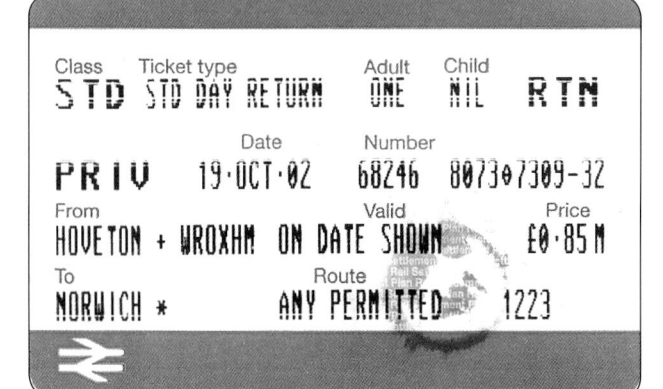

→ 32. No. 156409 accelerates away from the Bittern Line station with a Norwich to Sheringham train on 7th June 2012, as *Blickling Hall* awaits departure time with a train for Aylsham. The preserved signal box overlooks the scene. (R.J.Adderson)

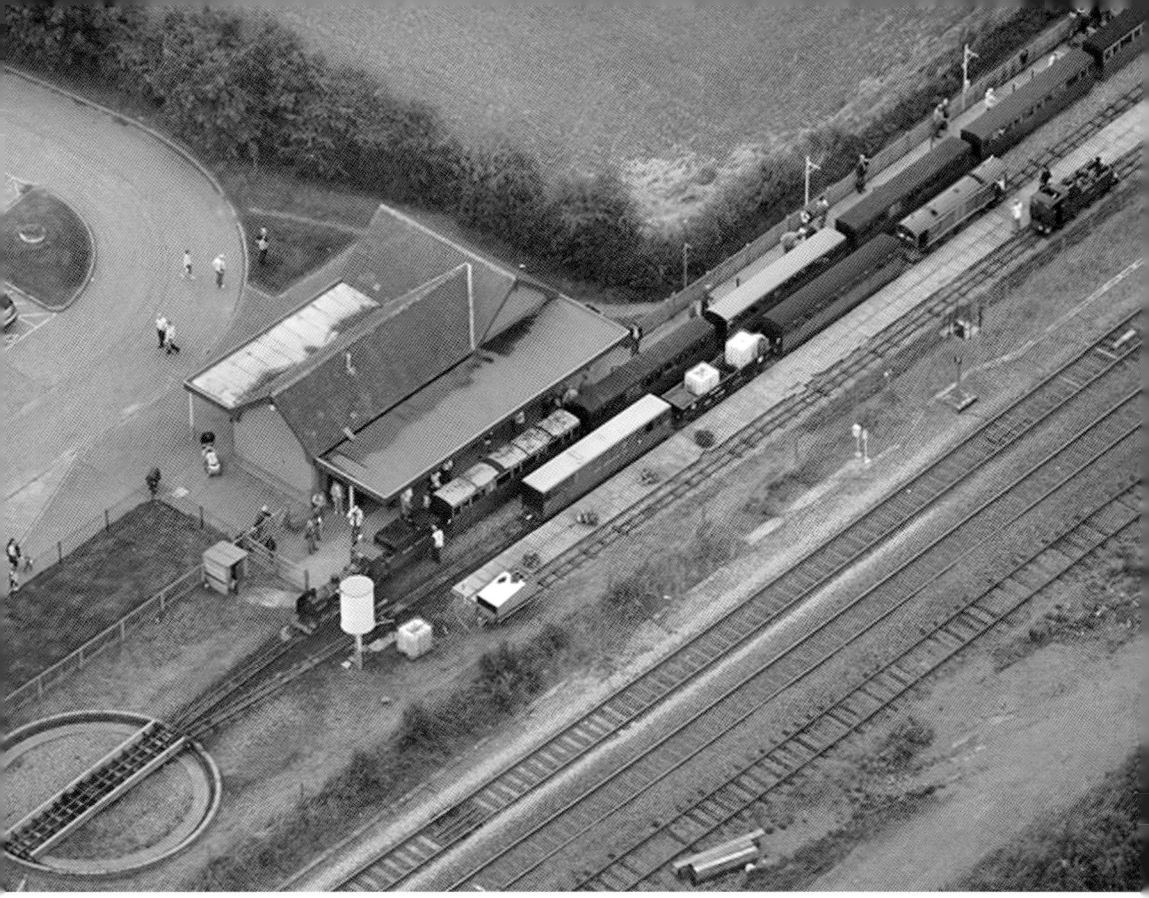

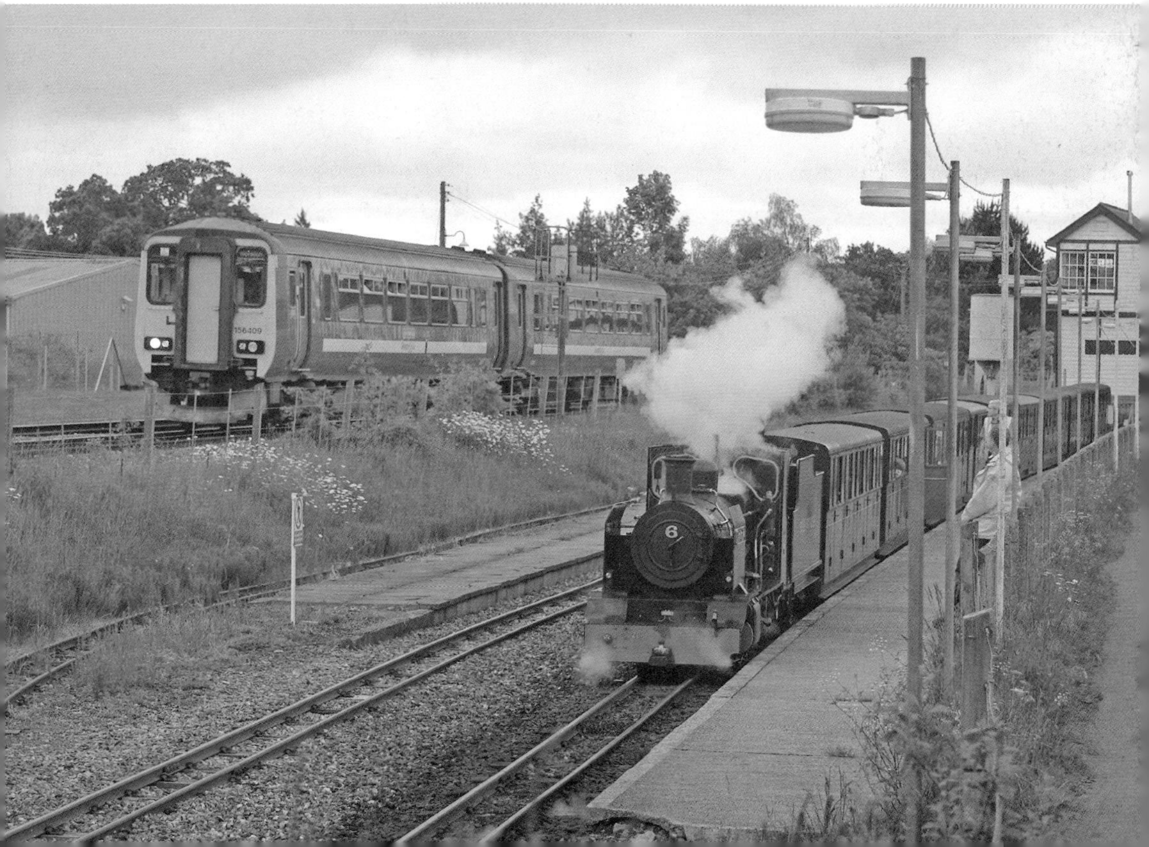
156409
6

NORTH OF WROXHAM

33. Although many of the level crossings on the line were converted to automatic barriers from 1967 onwards, some retained manually operated gates until the 2000 resignalling project was complete. Here is the open air ground frame at Sloley level crossing on 11th September 1999. The five levers control the crossing gates and the up and down home and distant signals which protected them. (S.McNae)

Handbill extract 1952.

				Day tour Tuesdays and Fridays only	Half-day tour Mondays to Saturdays inclusive
				a.m. a.m.	p.m. p.m.
Norwich (Thorpe)	...	...	... dep.	9 18 10 20	1 35**SX** 1 20**SO**
Whitlingham	...	...	,,	9 23 10 25	1 40**SX** 1 25**SO**
Wroxham (Rail)	...	...	... arr.	9 38 10 42	1 55**SX** 1 40**SO**
,, (Boat)	...	...	... dep.	11 0	3 15
				p.m.	
,, (Boat)	...	...	... arr.	5 30	5 45
,, (Rail)	...	...	... dep.	6 17 7 23	6 17 7 23
Whitlingham	...	...	... arr.	— 7 39	— 7 39
Norwich (Thorpe)	...	...	,,	6 33 7 44	6 33 7 44

WORSTEAD

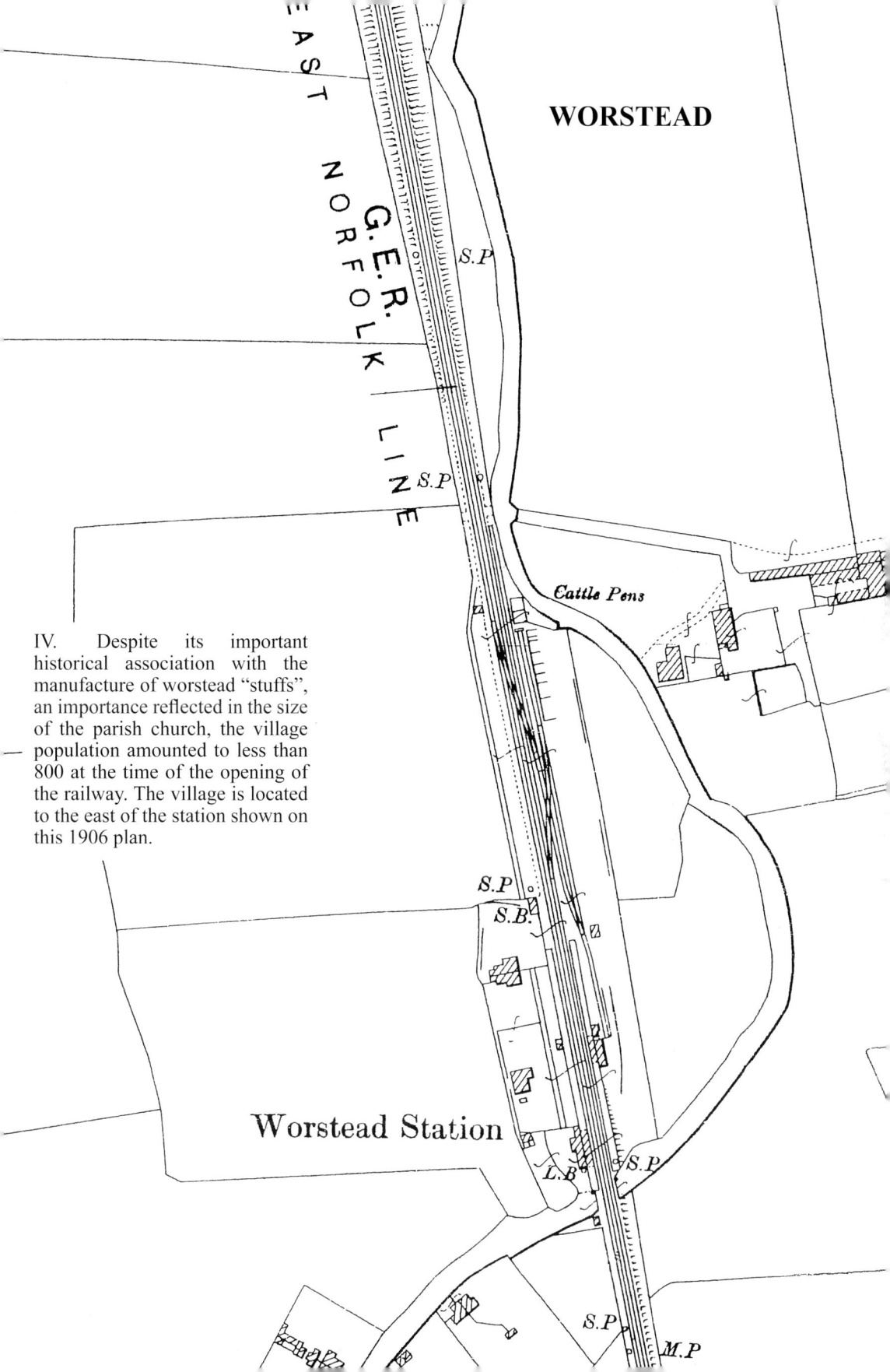

G.E.R. NORFOLK LINE

Cattle Pens

IV. Despite its important historical association with the manufacture of worstead "stuffs", an importance reflected in the size of the parish church, the village population amounted to less than 800 at the time of the opening of the railway. The village is located to the east of the station shown on this 1906 plan.

Worstead Station

34.   Seen from the signal box, class D27 2-2-2 no. 1008 heads north with an express passenger train. As the signalman is holding out the token for the single line section to North Walsham, we can see that the picture was taken before the line was converted to double track in 1901. The locomotive, built in 1893, is equipped for burning oil, rather than coal. (R.J.Adderson coll.)

→ 35. Now we are looking southwards to the station around 1960, with the tall GER signal dominating the scene, and a few wagons in the small goods yard to the left. Goods facilities were withdrawn in July 1964. (NRS Archive)

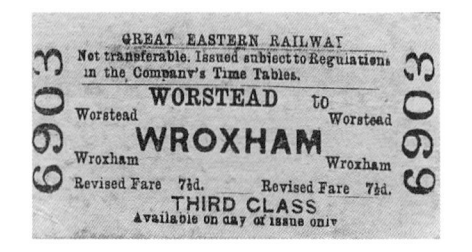

→ 36. As at Salhouse, the main buildings were on the down platform and of wooden construction, with a brick built waiting room on the opposite side. The facilities were completed by a gents toilet block set into the meticulously tended hedge. Further away, the signal box at the end of the platform remained in use until October 1964, when it was replaced by a 3-lever ground frame next to the manually operated level crossing gates. (NRS Archive)

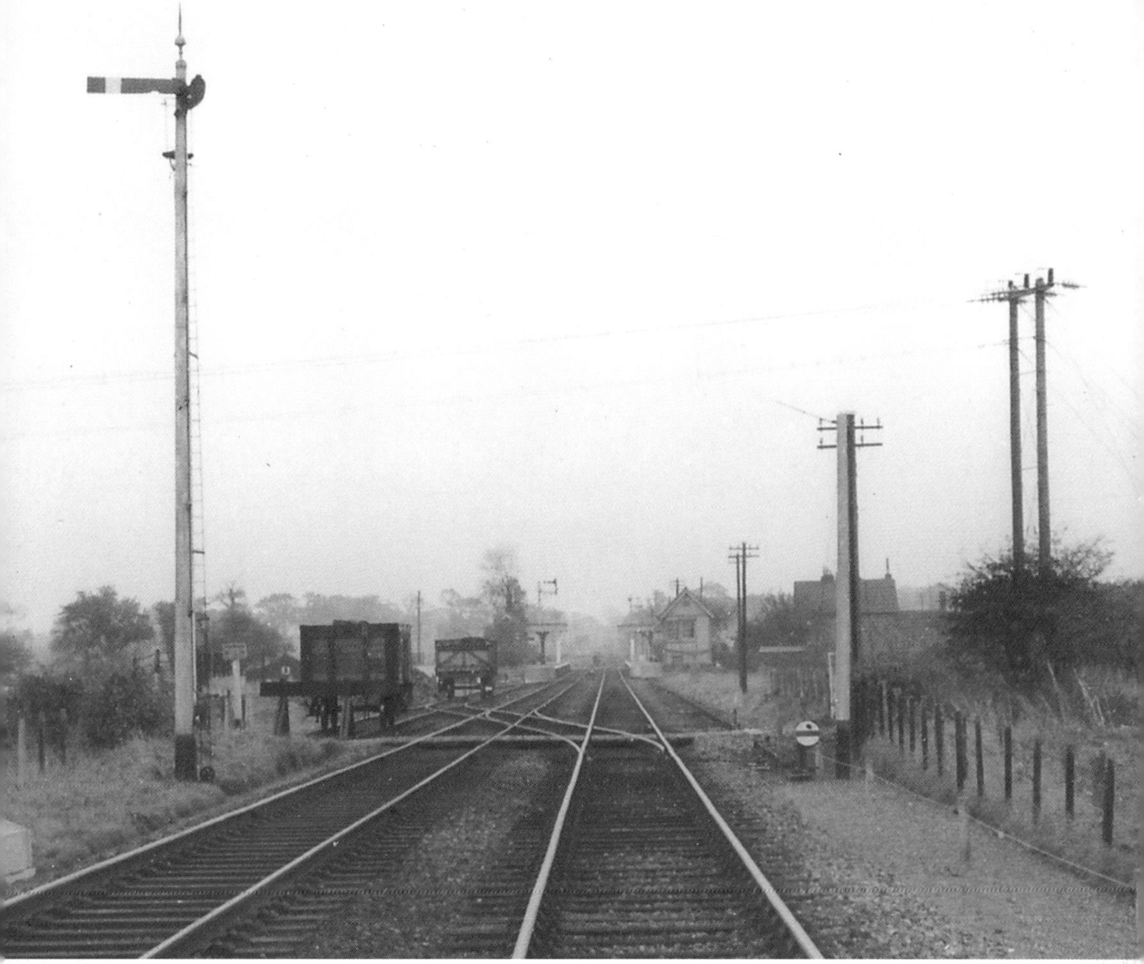

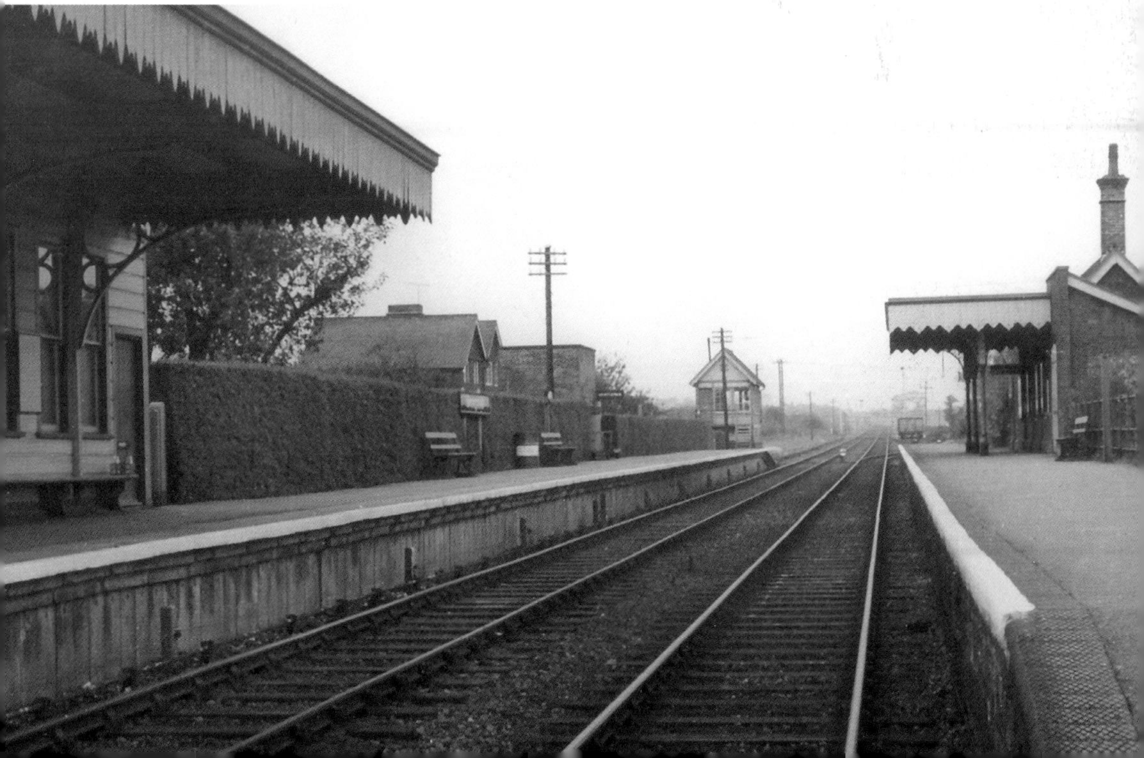

37.   This time we are looking towards Wroxham, again at a quiet period in the early 1960s, when the general appearance of the station had probably changed little over the previous 30 years. The signal arm is cantilevered outwards so that it is visible to the crews of approaching trains; a conventional design could have been hidden by the awning of the shelter. (Stations U.K.)

38.   When the line reverted to single track in January 1967, the former up line and platform were retained here. The redundant wooden building was soon demolished, but the shelter on the east side remained in 2012, as did the signal box, which had been purchased privately many years earlier. Having paused in the vain hope of attracting some custom, no. 156417 passes these survivors as it heads away towards North Walsham on 1st July 2012. (R.J.Adderson)

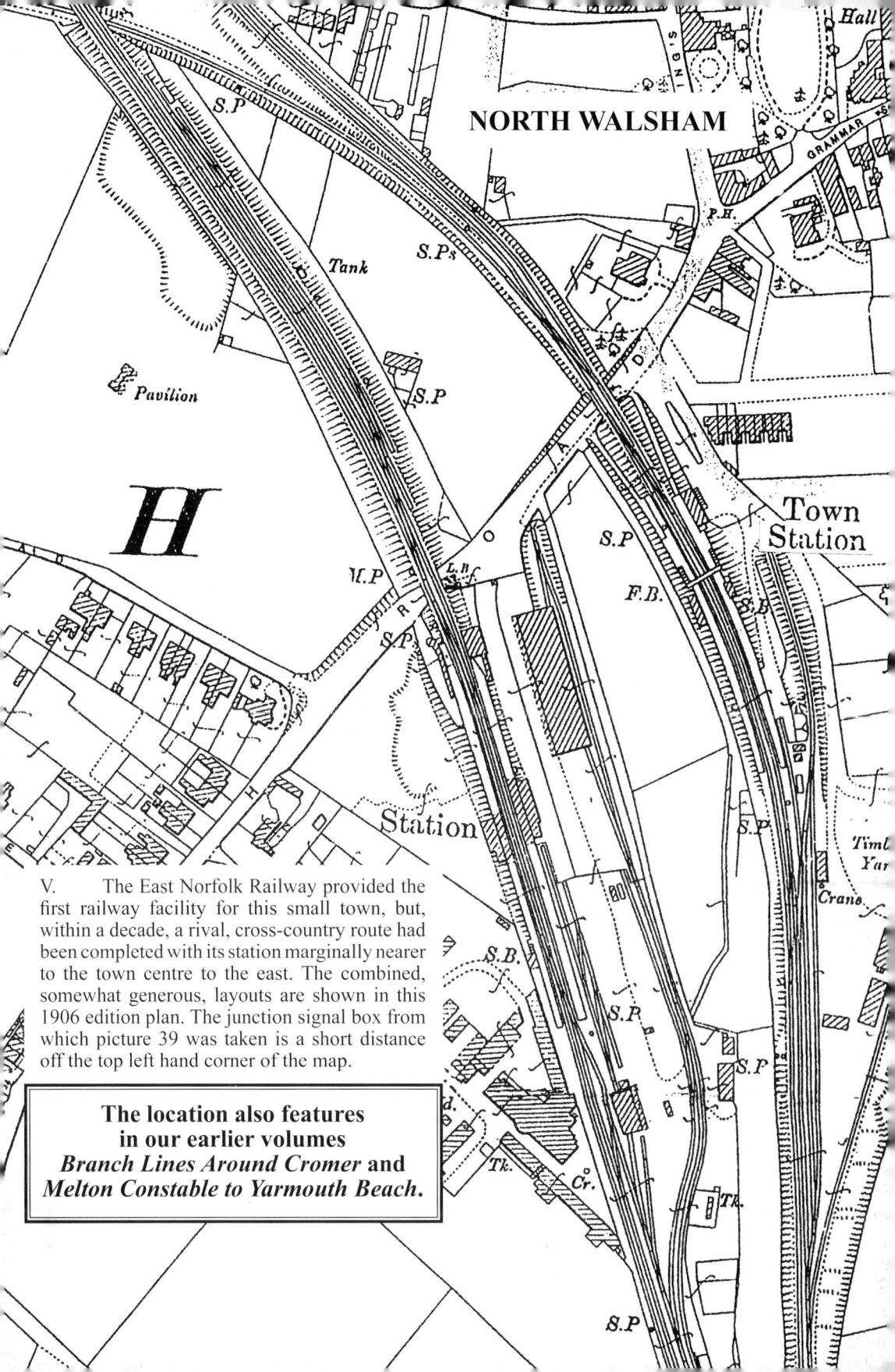

NORTH WALSHAM

V. The East Norfolk Railway provided the first railway facility for this small town, but, within a decade, a rival, cross-country route had been completed with its station marginally nearer to the town centre to the east. The combined, somewhat generous, layouts are shown in this 1906 edition plan. The junction signal box from which picture 39 was taken is a short distance off the top left hand corner of the map.

The location also features
in our earlier volumes
Branch Lines Around Cromer and
Melton Constable to Yarmouth Beach.

39. This picture, dating from 27th September 1911, illustrates part of the complex of railway lines to the north of the station. Our view is southwards from the signal box at the junction of the Mundesley branch, with the GER station just beyond the curve in the double track line. The single track of the M&GN main line swings sharply round from Town station to pass under the GER, while the line at top left provides a link from the M&GN to Antingham Road Junction, on the Mundesley branch. (GERS/Windwood coll.)

➔ 40. A second picture from that same day in 1911 is a view from the station signal box, looking south eastwards across the goods yard. There is plenty of traffic in the sidings, where the coal merchant is unloading the "Herbert Clarke" private owner wagon on to a horse drawn cart. The parallel M&GN line is hidden behind the trees at the edge of the yard. (GERS/Windwood coll.)

➔ 41. Class L1 2-6-4T no. 67707 arrives with the 5.18 pm train from Norwich to Melton Constable on Saturday 7th September 1957. The train is full of people returning home, either after a day's shopping in the city, or maybe having watched Norwich City beat Brentford 3-1 in the Third Division South that afternoon. (B.Harrison)

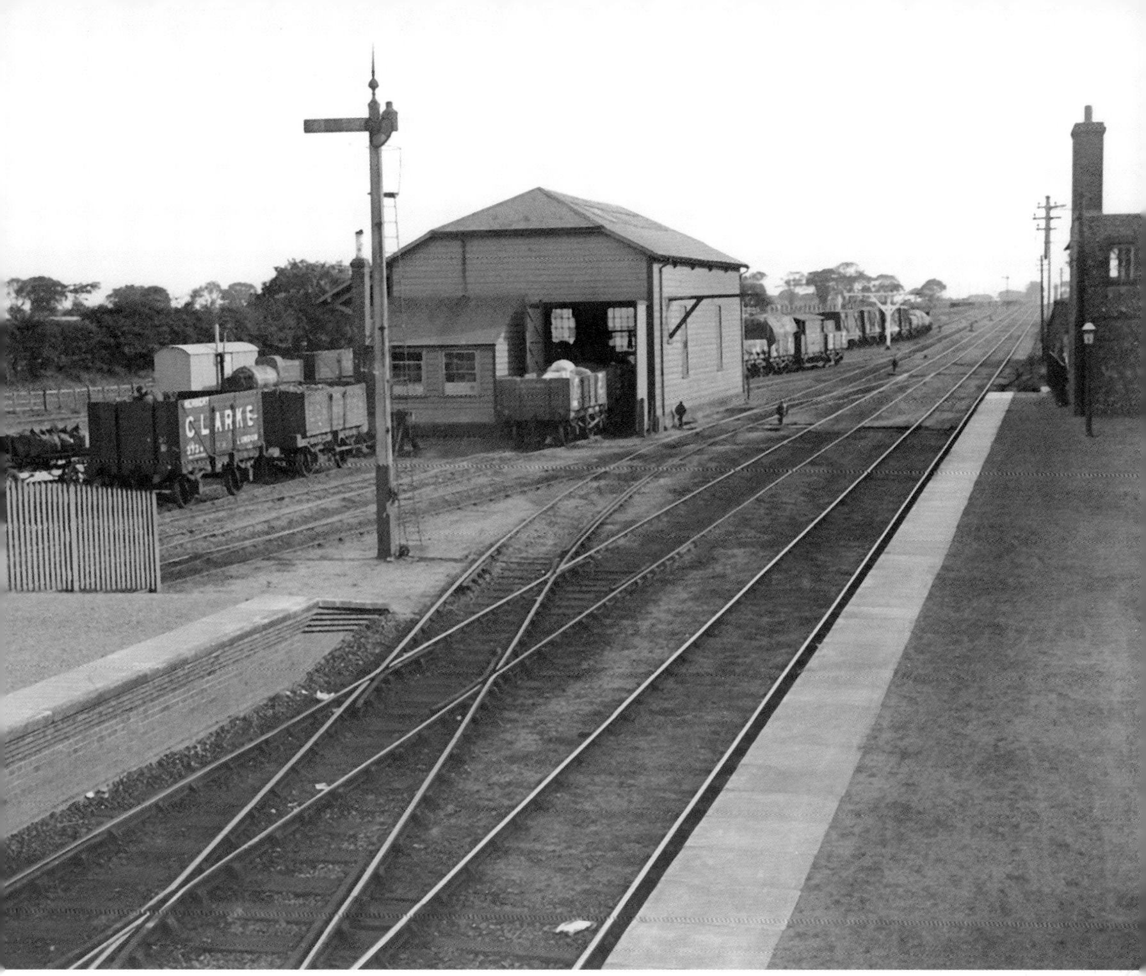
CLARKE

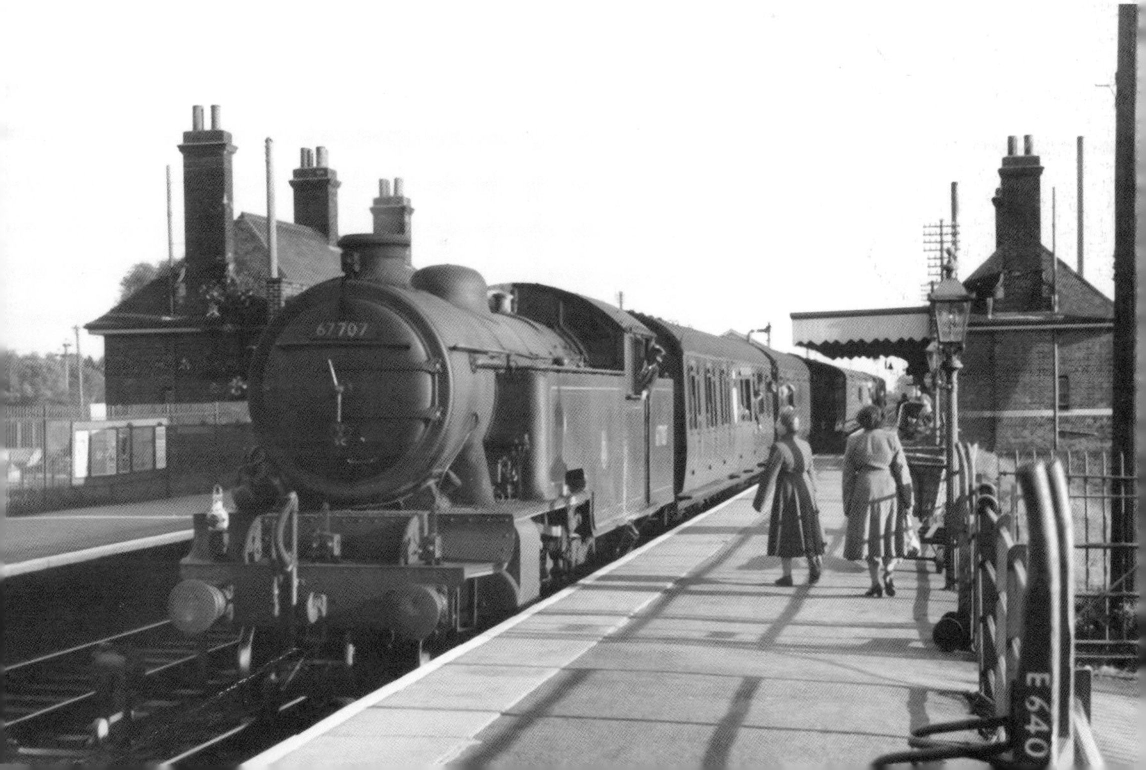
67707
E 640

42. As we have seen in picture 39, the two railways here were for many years connected by a line between Antingham Road Junction and the M&GN station. The poor condition of a bridge led to this line being taken out of use during the Spring of 1958, to be replaced by a new connecting line some 300 yards south of the GER station, at a point where the former rival lines ran parallel. It saw little use, as the M&GN line was closed completely on 28th February 1959, although the goods yard at Town station continued in use for a few more years afterwards. A DMU from Norwich passes the new connection, while another train is signalled on the M&GN route.
(I.C.Allen/Transport Treasury)

➔ 43. Railborne freight traffic was in major decline in the late 1960s, especially in rural areas, but the thriving yard at North Walsham was an exception to this trend. A Brush type 2 diesel has arrived with a goods train in April 1969, and the front two wagons, laden with steel girders, will be shunted into the yard, while the coal wagons are bound for Cromer. The blue running-in board proclaims "North Walsham Main", the suffix having been added at nationalisation to differentiate from the M&GN's "North Walsham Town" station. (G.H.Smith)

➔ 44. It is 13th April 1970 and there are two trains of Freightliner flats, loaded with containers, in the goods yard, as yet more containers arrive on lorries from the factory. Containers were revolutionising freight transport at this time, and many hundreds were built at a factory in the town and taken out by rail to meet the demands of the freight handling industry. Adding to this busy scene, there is conventional goods traffic in the siding on the right, where a lorry is being loaded with what appears to be road chippings. While all this was going on, two new sidings were being laid to the east of the yard to handle the condensate traffic from Bacton. (G.H.Smith)

7K02
NORTH WALSHAM
MAIN

Seatrain
Seatrain
Seatrain
Seatrain

45.   This is the gated approach to the compound enclosing the new sidings on 25th February 1990, with a class 31 backing on to the loaded tank wagons. Over the years, locomotives of classes 37, either singly or in pairs, 47 and 58 have also appeared on these trains. The new class 66s appeared in 1999, and quickly established a monopoly of the workings. (D.C.Pearce)

46.   After being under threat for some time, the platform buildings were demolished in 1998, and were replaced with shelters incorporating some of the old awnings and ironwork. Sadly, these lasted for only a few years and were themselves replaced by considerably more basic structures, as seen here on 7th May 2012. No. 156402 leaves platform 2 with a train for Sheringham, as passengers for Norwich wait for no. 156416 to come to a standstill. We will now join them, and retrace our steps back to Wroxham, for a journey over the branch line to County School. (R.J.Adderson)

2. Wroxham to County School
WEST OF WROXHAM

47. A mile or so west of Wroxham, we come to the ungated level crossing at Belaugh Green, where the railway meets a minor country lane, and there can be no doubt that we are now travelling along a quiet rural branch line. The crossing keeper's cottage is prominent in this view, looking westwards from the brake van of a goods train on 9th July 1969, and suggests that the crossing had been attended in years gone by. (Railway Record of the British Isles/G.L.Pring)

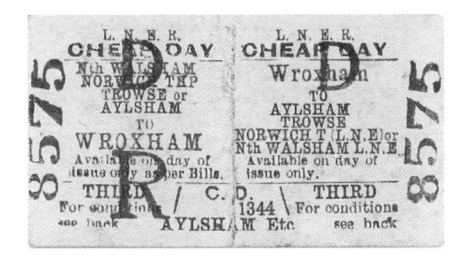

COLTISHALL

VI. Work started on the Royal Air Force base of the same name in 1939. Following tradition, it should have been named after the nearest railway station which was, in fact, Buxton Lamas; but to avoid possible confusion with Buxton in Derbyshire, "RAF Coltishall" was chosen. The map dates from the previous year.

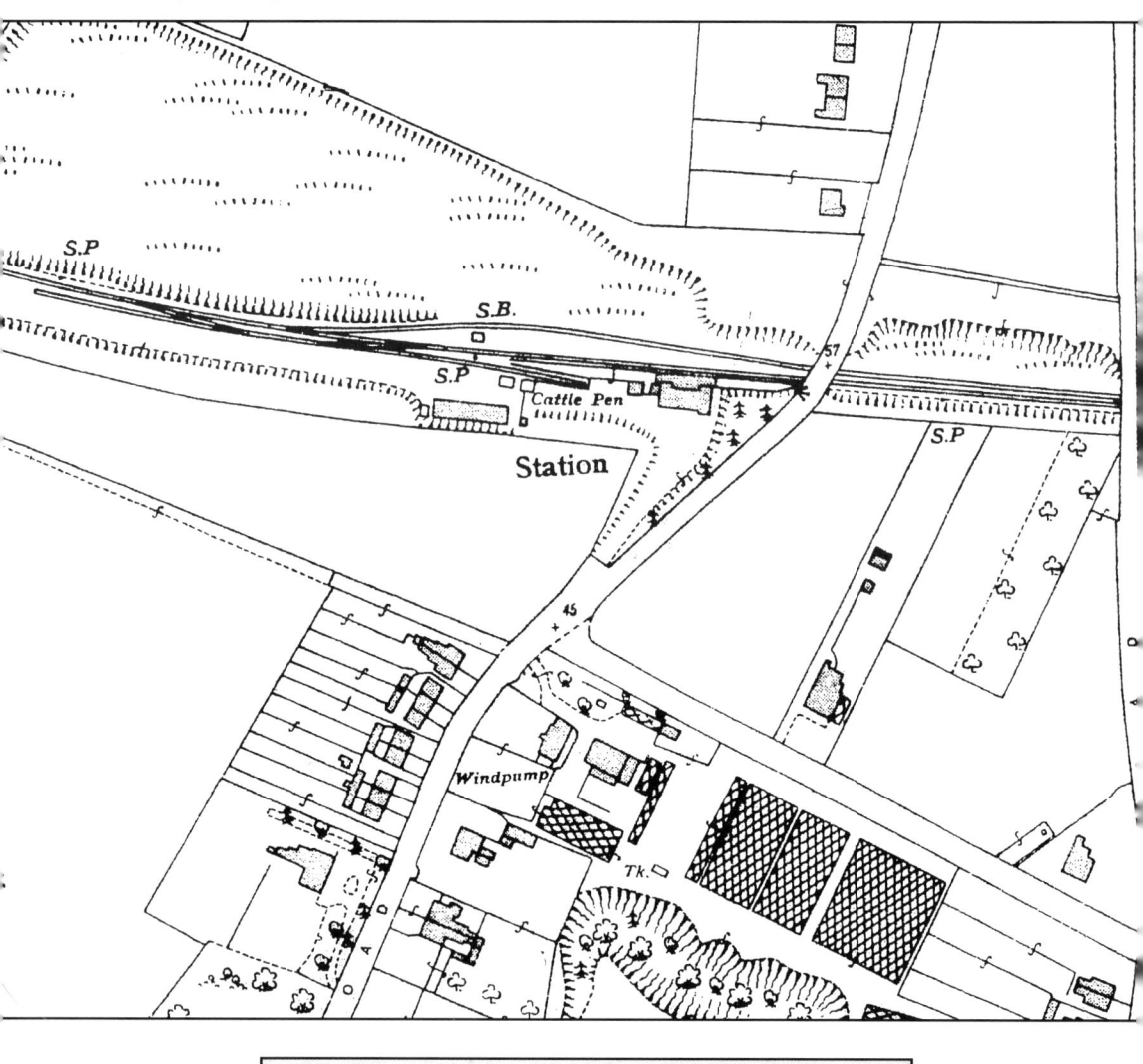

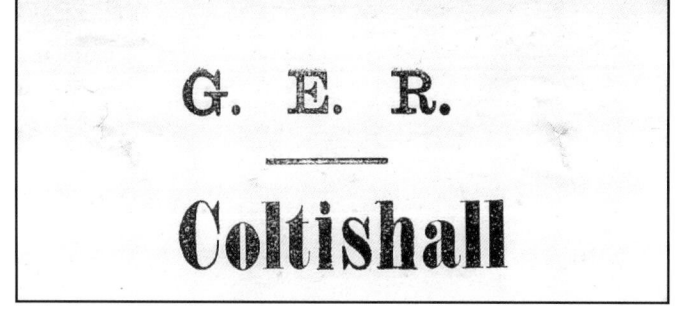

G. E. R.

Coltishall

48. The station was approached by a driveway from the road, and was of a similar design to the others on the branch, with a single storey station building adjoining the station master's house. This was the scene in the early years of the 20th century, and in essence there had been little external change to the building in 2012, when it was providing Bed and Breakfast accommodation. (A.R.Taylor coll.)

49. The station master stands on the platform with his family and two uniformed members of the staff. Meanwhile, the men working on the track seem unsure whether to pose for the cameraman or to continue with their labours. Again, the picture dates from the years before World War I, when the building was liberally coated with ivy. (G.Gosling coll.)

50. We move forward some 50 years, to find class J17 0-6-0 no. 65519 shunting the wagons of the daily goods train on 3rd May 1958. It would appear that a wagonload of coal has been left in the siding to the right. The photographer is looking out of the signal box, towards Buxton Lamas. (R.Harrison)

➔ 51. The west end of the station had a busy air about it as late as 3rd August 1961. Wagons are dotted about in the sidings, as a Brush type 2 approaches with a goods train. The signal box is still there, although it is "switched out", and the signals are clear in each direction. However, it was destined to be closed and demolished within the next year or so.
(J.Watling)

➔ 52. Although general goods facilities were withdrawn in April 1965, the loop siding was revived on two separate occasions later in the decade. Firstly, there was the sand traffic for Pointers, excavated locally and destined for Beddington Lane, near Croydon. A pair of BTH type 2 (later class 15) diesels accelerate the loaded wagons through the station, having left a rake of empty wagons in the siding. At a time when private owner wagons were something of a rarity, Pointers owned a fleet of 75 ex-SNCF wagons registered for main line running. Many of these carried the company's logo and were marked "Return to Coltishall". This traffic flow began in 1966 but had ceased by the autumn of 1968, when the trains were being loaded at Drayton on the M&GN.
(I.C.Allen/Transport Treasury)

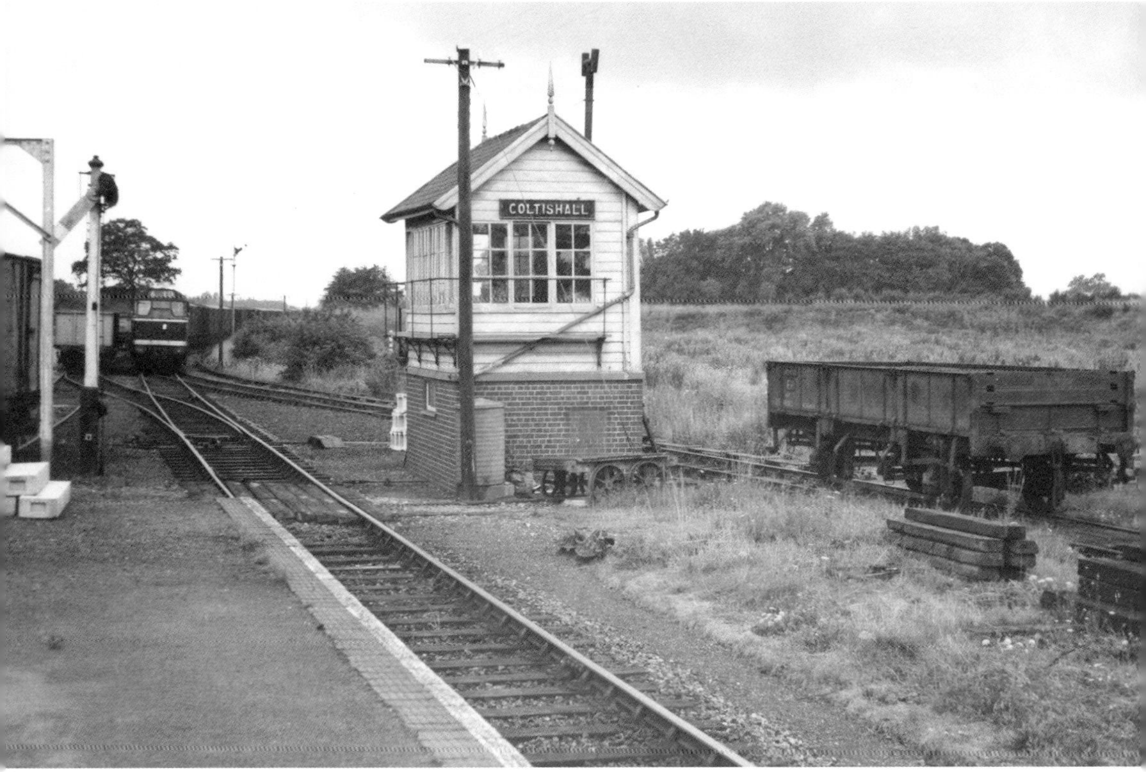
COLTISHALL

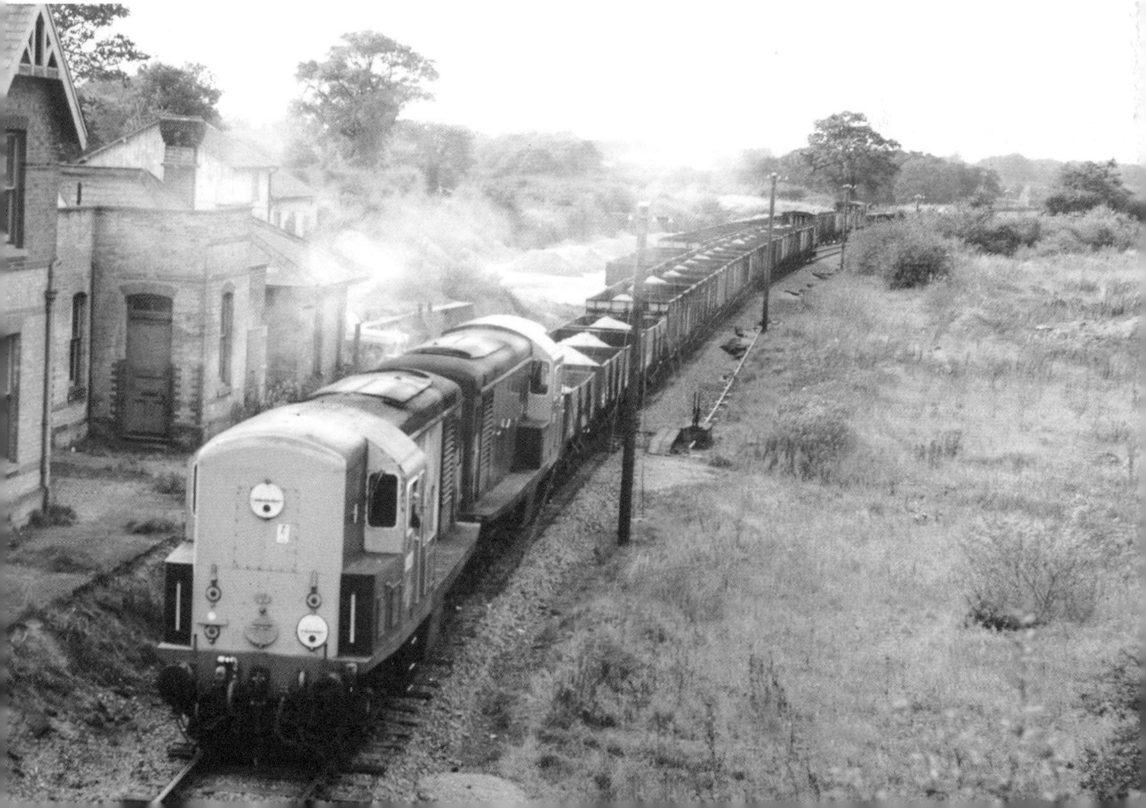

53. After the sand traffic ceased, the siding saw further use for loading condensate from Bacton gas works, which had opened in 1968. This was a temporary measure during 1969 and 1970 pending completion of the loading facility at North Walsham, which we saw in picture 45. A rake of wagons for this traffic is being loaded from road tankers as no. D5657 runs past. Health and safety requirements are seemingly satisfied by a crude "No Smoking" notice nailed to an apparently home-made "No Admittance" sign.
(I.C.Allen/Transport Treasury)

➜ 54. The GER station building dominates the background as a Bure Valley train runs into the loop on 5th May 2012. Part of the old platform had been demolished in the 1960s to enable the loop to be extended for the sand traffic, revealing the wall of the former loading dock to the right of the picture.
(R.J.Adderson)

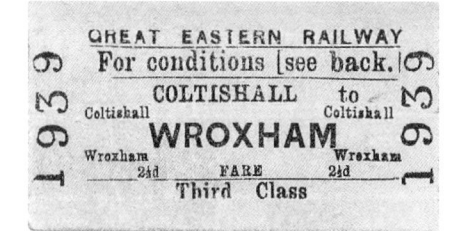

➜ 55. Seen from the edge of the old loading dock, no. 7 *Spitfire* passes the concrete island platform of the narrow gauge station with a train from Aylsham on 5th May 2012. The footpath to the left of the railway is very much on the line of the loop siding which appears in picture 53.
(R.J.Adderson)

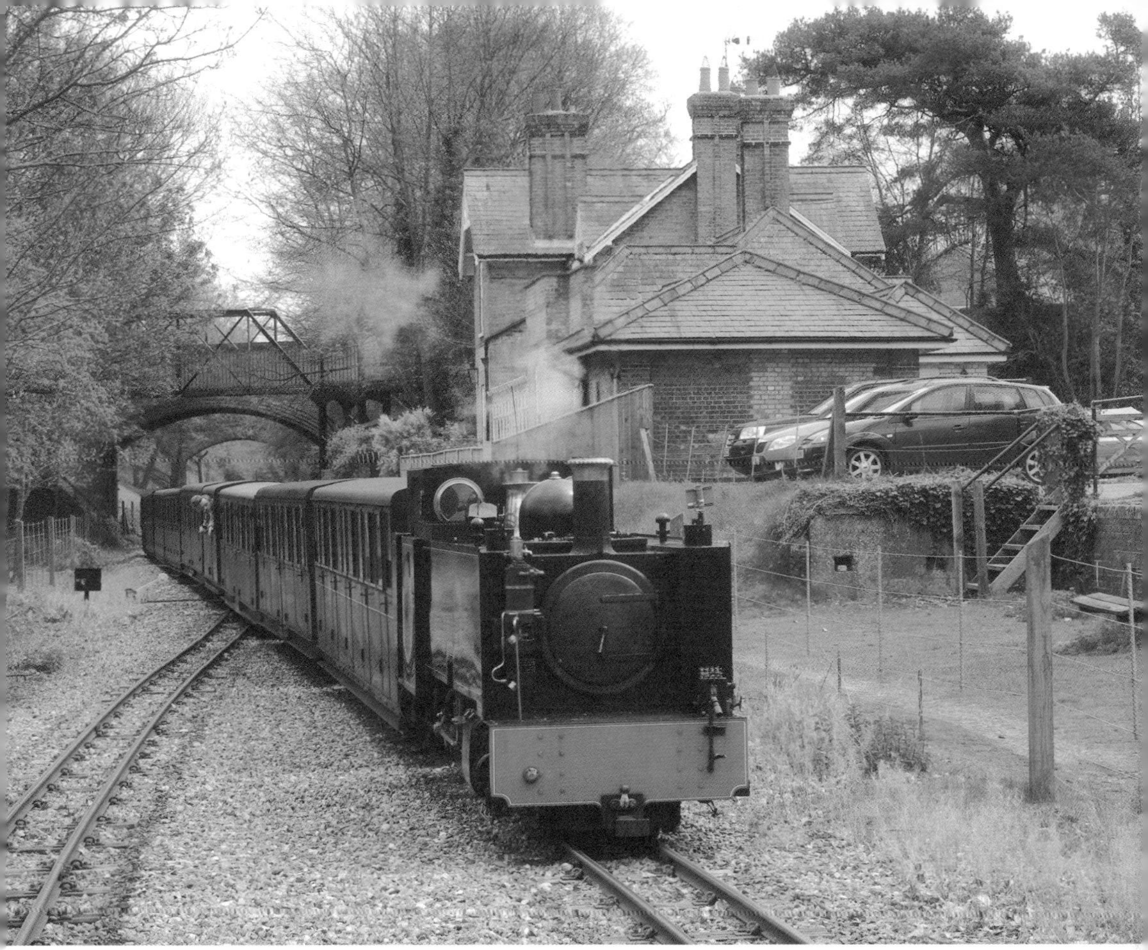

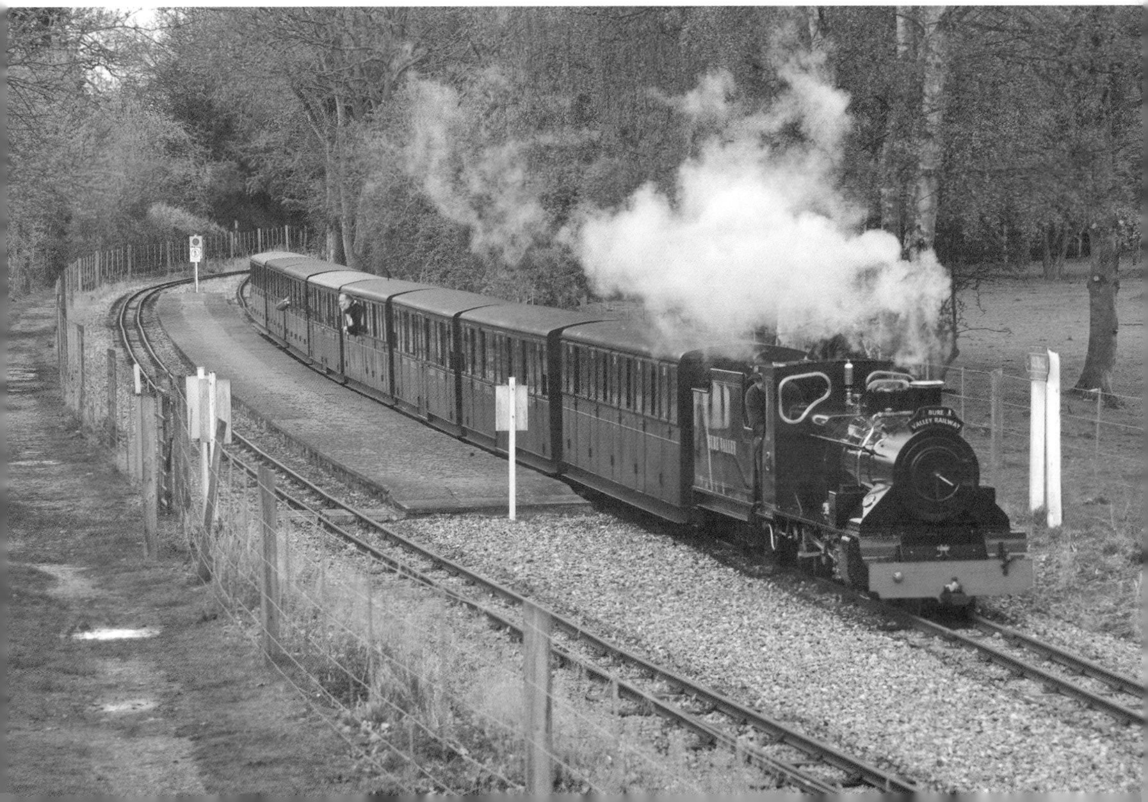

WEST OF COLTISHALL

56.   Three passing loops provide operating flexibility on the narrow gauge line. The middle one of these was built at Hautbois, a remote spot in the meadows close to the river. No.6 *Blickling Hall* waits in the loop as a train from Wroxham approaches behind no.1 *Wroxham Broad* on 30th July 2011. (R.J.Adderson)

```
              CENTENARY TRAIN
           R·D·S/A·D·R·A·C SPECIAL

          REEPHAM              SATURDAY
                              MAY 2nd, 1981
              CAWSTON
                  AYLSHAM
                     BUXTON
      Return              COLTISHALL
      ADULT £2.50
      CHILD £1.75              NORWICH
```

EAST OF BUXTON LAMAS

57. We are looking across the bridge over the River Bure towards Buxton Lamas on 8th July 1969, with the tower of the village church in the distance. Although the river ran broadly parallel to the railway between Wroxham and Aylsham, it was only rarely visible to passengers. In later years, the bridge structure was ingeniously adapted to carry both the 15" gauge line and the adjacent footpath. (Railway Record of the British Isles/G.L.Pring)

G. E. R.

Buxton Lamas

BUXTON LAMAS

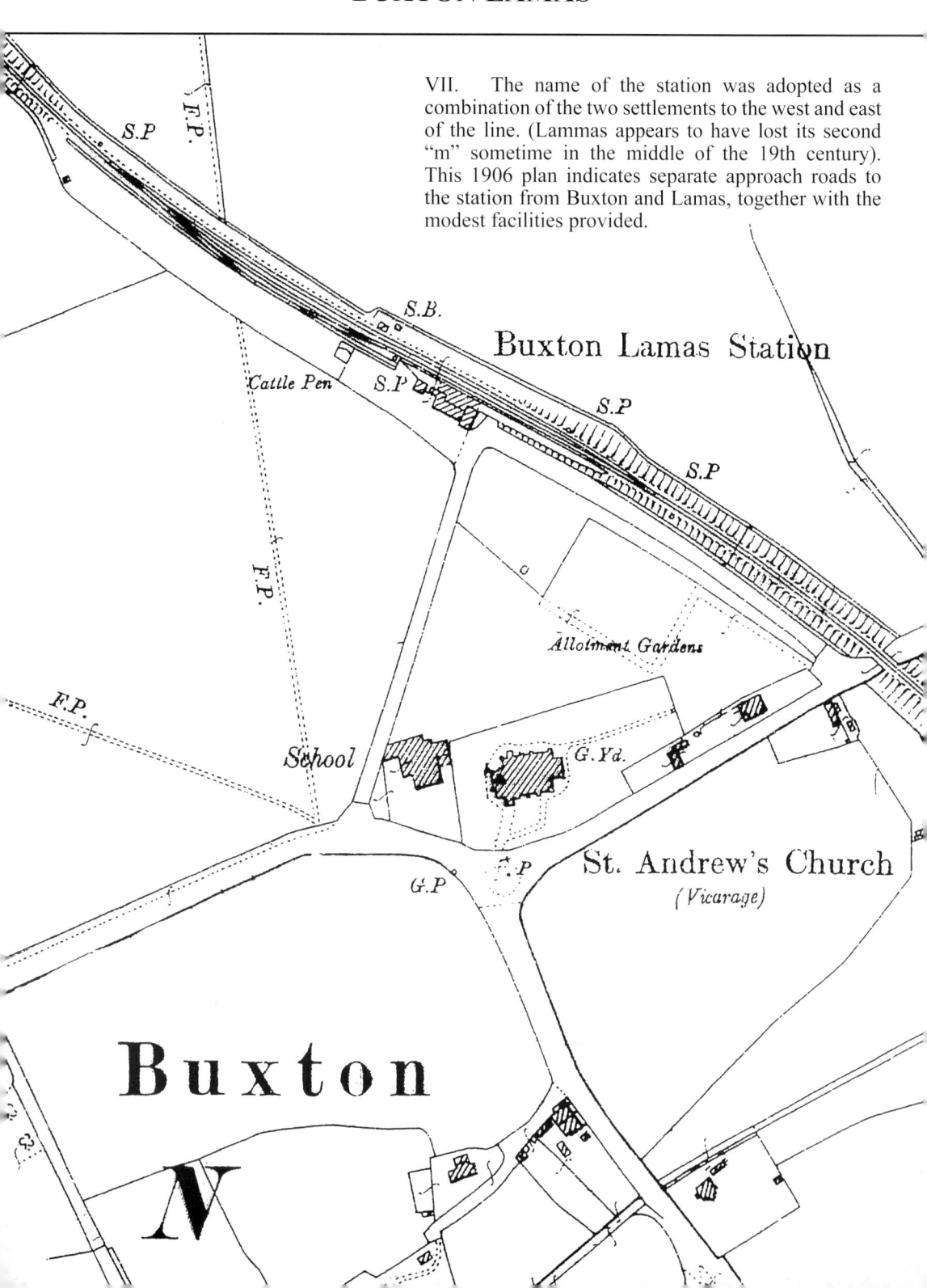

VII. The name of the station was adopted as a combination of the two settlements to the west and east of the line. (Lammas appears to have lost its second "m" sometime in the middle of the 19th century). This 1906 plan indicates separate approach roads to the station from Buxton and Lamas, together with the modest facilities provided.

58. Three smartly dressed young men pose by the nameboard at Buxton Lamas, probably during the 1930s. When the railway came, Buxton and Lamas were two separate, but adjoining, parishes, each with its own church, post office, school and public house. It was common enough for railway companies to incorporate two place names in their station titles, but usually they would be separated by "And" or "For". (Suffolk Record Office Ipswich Branch, K681/2/86/63)

59. By the Summer of 1959 the line was handling just one goods train daily, and there is a deserted look to the station. The main running line is still shiny, but the loop siding is black with rust, having been disused since the previous September. Oddly, the cast iron "Gentleman" sign is still in place, a peculiar survival that was repeated at other places along the line. (R.J.Adderson)

60. One of the familiar Brush type 2 diesels heads west through the station on 2nd August 1961. By now, traffic had increased with the opening of the connecting line at Themelthorpe, and this train was bound for Norwich City station. We can see that the signal has been replaced by a considerably shorter version since the previous picture was taken. (J.Watling)

➔ 61. We are looking along the approach road to the station on 8th June 1963. The building here is very similar in design to that at Coltishall, with the single storey sections at both these locations being smaller than those at the stations further west. In later years the building served for a while as an annexe to the nearby village school but later reverted to private use. (B.W.L Brooksbank)

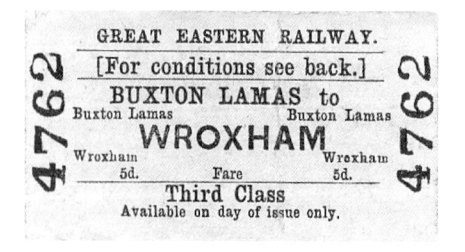

➔ 62. The early 1960s saw a rapid decline; the disused loop siding was lifted in 1961/2 and the signal box was abolished during 1962, leaving the remaining sidings to be worked from a two lever ground frame until goods facilities were withdrawn from 19th April 1965. Little more than a year later, on 30th April 1966, there was just a single track through the platform, although the locations of the sidings and the brick foundations of the signal box were still evident. (M.D.Rayner)

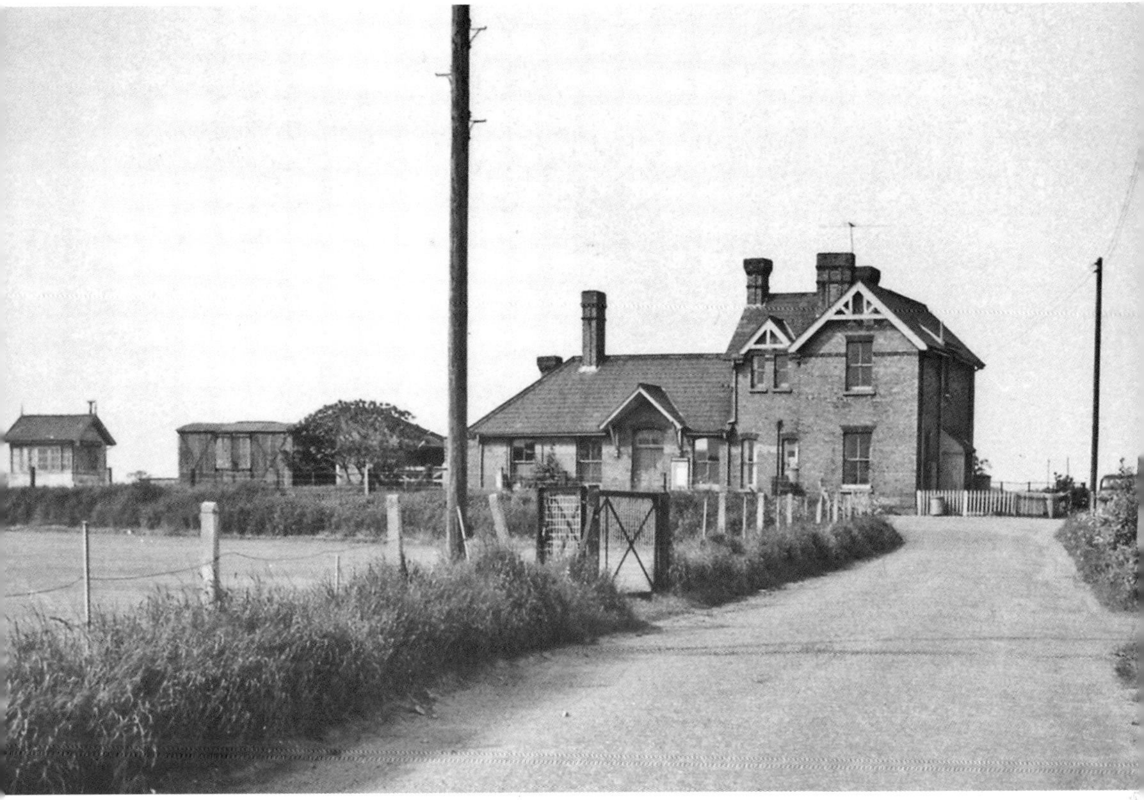

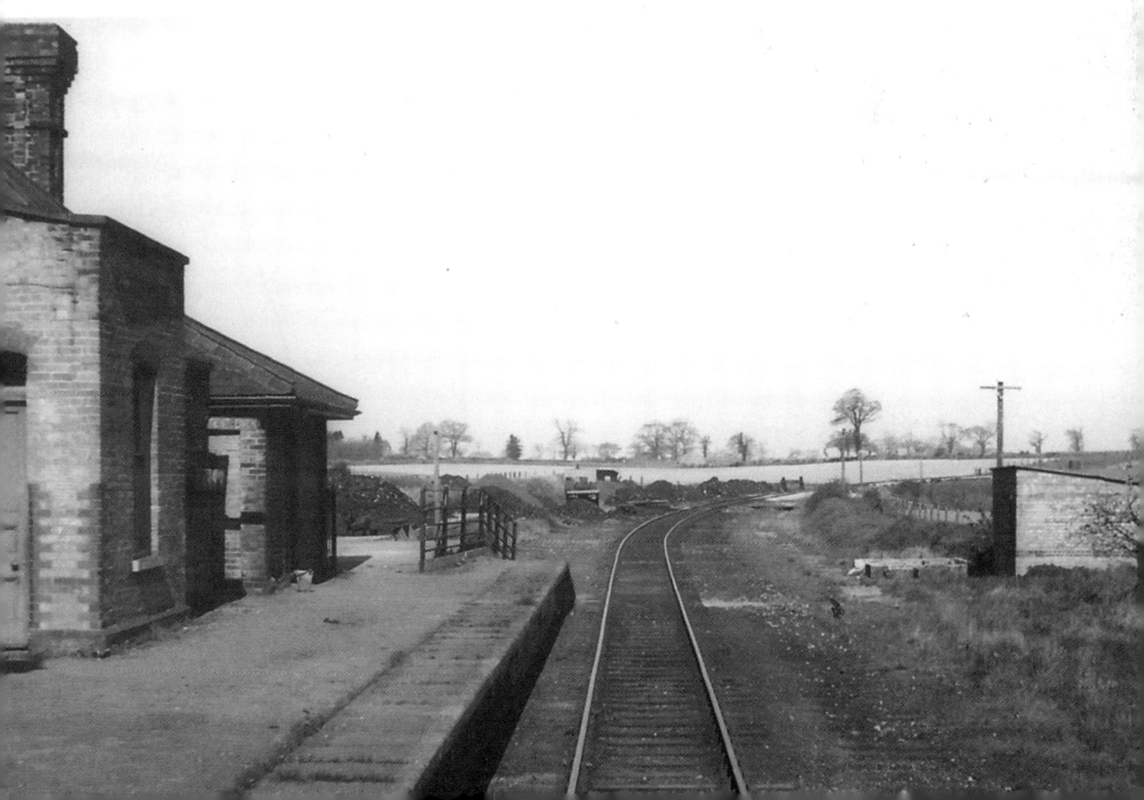

63.   A Bure Valley Railway train is dwarfed by the former station building as it heads for Aylsham on 2nd June 2012. The photographer is standing close to the site of the signal box, while the course of the loop siding is now the route of the public footpath. (R.J.Adderson)

64.   After making a request stop at the station, the driver of no. 6 *Blickling Hall* acknowledges the guard's "Right Away" signal and turns back into the cab, ready to continue his journey westwards on 1st July 2012. The Bure Valley Railway stopping place is a simple concrete pad with a couple of seats, brightened by a colourful display of flowers on this Summer afternoon. (R.J.Adderson)

WEST OF BUXTON LAMAS

65. The third passing loop on the narrow-gauge line was installed close to the village of Brampton, roughly midway between Buxton Lamas and Aylsham. A small platform was constructed beside the single track just west of the loop, thus putting the village on the railway map for the first time. We can see that the facilities are fairly basic, as no. 8 runs through the platform with a train for Wroxham on 2nd June 2012. It is difficult to believe that this sylvan setting was an exposed stretch of embankment in standard gauge days. (R.J.Adderson)

1990 SUMMER TIMETABLE

AYLSHAM–WROXHAM
Trains depart at:

9.00 am	1.32 pm
10.08 am	2.40 pm
11.16 am	3.48 pm
12.24 pm	4.56 pm

WROXHAM–AYLSHAM
Trains depart at:

10.08 am	2.40 pm
11.16 am	3.48 pm
12.24 pm	4.56 pm
1.32 pm	6.04 pm

Daily service from early July to late October.
Journey time: 40 minutes.
Timetable subject to change without prior notice.

1990 first summer of operation.

EAST OF AYLSHAM

66. A special train formed by the Eastern Region General Manager's saloon waits at Greenwood level crossing, half a mile or so east of Aylsham station, as a member of the train crew opens the gates to enable it to proceed. At the time, 20th July 1974, this was one of the two remaining gated crossings between Wroxham and Reepham. The former crossing keeper's cottage is prominent on the far side of the line. (R.J.Adderson)

67. The same building features in this picture, but the country lane now forms part of the recently constructed Aylsham by-pass. A DMU special causes minimal delay to road traffic on 2nd May 1981 as it heads for Aylsham. Running from Norwich to Reepham and back, this proved to be the final passenger train over the branch. (R.J.Adderson)

68. Completing the transformation, a train emerges from the tunnel which takes the 15ins gauge line safely under the busy bypass. It is 23rd August 1990, and the engine *Winston Churchill* is on loan from the Romney Hythe & Dymchurch Railway for the first season of BVR operation. The crossing cottage still provides the backdrop to a much changed scene. (R.J.Adderson)

G. E. R.

Aylsham

AYLSHAM

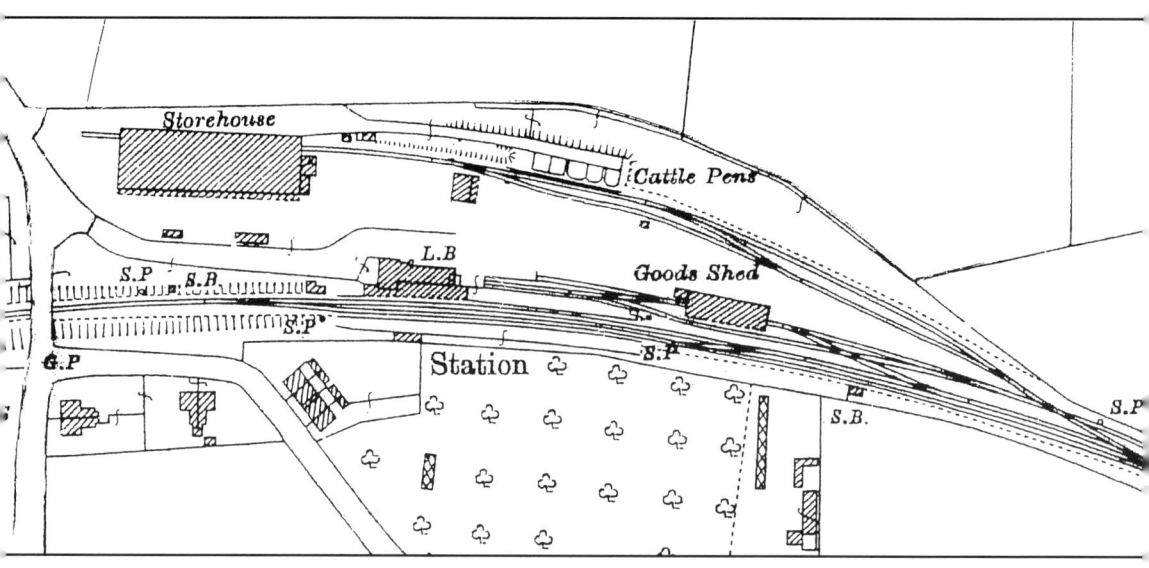

VIII. The opening westwards from Buxton Lamas took place on New Years Day 1880. This took place with permission from the Board of Trade, but prior to the formal inspection; Major General Hutchinson, who was due to carry out the inspection and who had authorised the opening of the Tay Bridge in 1878, was required at the latter, following the disaster on 28th December 1879. He had however, managed to visit Aylsham by the 8th January 1880. Prior to the extension westwards to Cawston in September of the same year the single up platform had been sufficient. The map indicates the facilities as they existed in 1928.

69. This postcard is dated 1880, and goes back to the eight month period during which the station was a terminus, before the line was extended to Cawston. A tank engine is running round its train, prior to working back to Wroxham, and the southern platform has not yet been built. Between July and December 1879 trains had run between Wroxham and Buxton Lamas only, and during this time it was recorded that "Stapleton's conveyance" provided Aylsham with a connection to the trains at Buxton Lamas. "Stapleton" was the memorably named Christmas Stapleton, licensee of the town's Black Boys Hotel, and the "conveyance" was no doubt horse drawn.
(Aylsham Town Archive)

70. Here we have another view from much the same angle, looking eastwards from the road bridge in Great Eastern days. There are now two platforms, and the large goods shed is prominent at the far end of the station. Two horses are being led down the station approach road behind the fencing, and beyond them are the coal office of R Coller and the white painted cattle pens, catering for two very important types of traffic. (P.Standley coll.)

71. We are now looking in the other direction, probably during the 1930s, and the station has a prosperous air about it, belying the fact that it handled no more than three or four passenger trains a day in each direction. The canopy extends the full length of the building, and is supported by substantial timber stanchions, similar in design to those we have already seen at Coltishall and Buxton Lamas. (Stations UK)

72. We now move forward to British Railways days as a rather leaky class E4 2-4-0 heads its three coach train away from the station stop. There have been a lot of detail changes since picture 70 was taken, and the pillbox on the embankment is a reminder of the turmoil that the world had gone through during the same period. On 27th September 1948, the station was officially renamed "Aylsham South", while the town's former M&GN station gained the "North" title at the same time. (I.C.Allen/Transport Treasury)

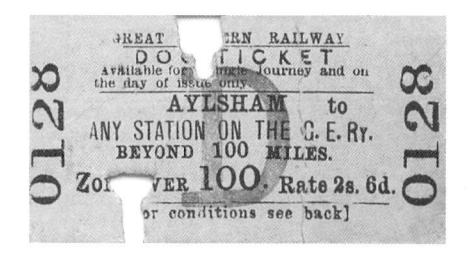

73. The first passenger train for over eight years arrived on 8th October 1960, when class B12 4-6-0 no 61572 paused with a railtour, in the course of a circuitous journey from Norwich City to Norwich Thorpe. There is time for the participants to explore their surroundings, whilst the photographer has chosen the signal box for his vantage point. Later in its journey, the train made a further photo stop at Coltishall, where the engine came to a stand under the road bridge next to a line of wagons stabled in the adjacent siding, thus limiting the pictorial opportunities available to the passengers. (M. Fordham)

74. A Brush type 2 diesel passes the neat little signal box on 20th April 1963. Goods traffic over the line had increased after the Themelthorpe spur opened in 1960, and three years later the Working Timetable showed two trains each day running between the two Norwich stations, together with an "as required" return journey to serve the concrete works at Lenwade. The needs of the intermediate stations were met by a pick up goods train from Wensum sidings (Norwich) to Reepham and back, running on Mondays, Wednesdays and Fridays. (W.J.Naunton)

75. Like the station buildings, the goods shed was a solidly built structure. Here we see the "road" side of the shed, looking towards Buxton Lamas on 23rd August 1965. There are three loading bays set in the north wall, each with an individual shelter offering workmen some protection from the elements, while steps from ground level lead up to the adjoining office building. (G.Pember)

➔ 76. The mid 1960s saw most of the branch lines in East Anglia reduced to "basic railways", with the widespread withdrawal of station staff, while track rationalisation and the disappearance of goods yards at the country stations led to the demolition of many small signal boxes. Aylsham was a rare exception to this trend, retaining a traditional atmosphere as late as 20th June 1967, with its signals, loop and goods traffic. The signal box was eventually closed in December 1973, but the sidings and loop remained until May 1977.
(Railway Record of the British Isles/G.L.Pring)

➔ 77. A number of special passenger trains visited the line between 1972 and its closure. One of these was "The Broadsman", organised by the Lea Valley Railway Club, which was formed of non-corridor coaches and ran through from Moorgate (London) to Lenwade, with occasional "comfort stops" on the way. The participants take the opportunity of stretching their legs and photographing no. 31160 during the Aylsham stop on 2nd October 1976. (M.J.Wilson)

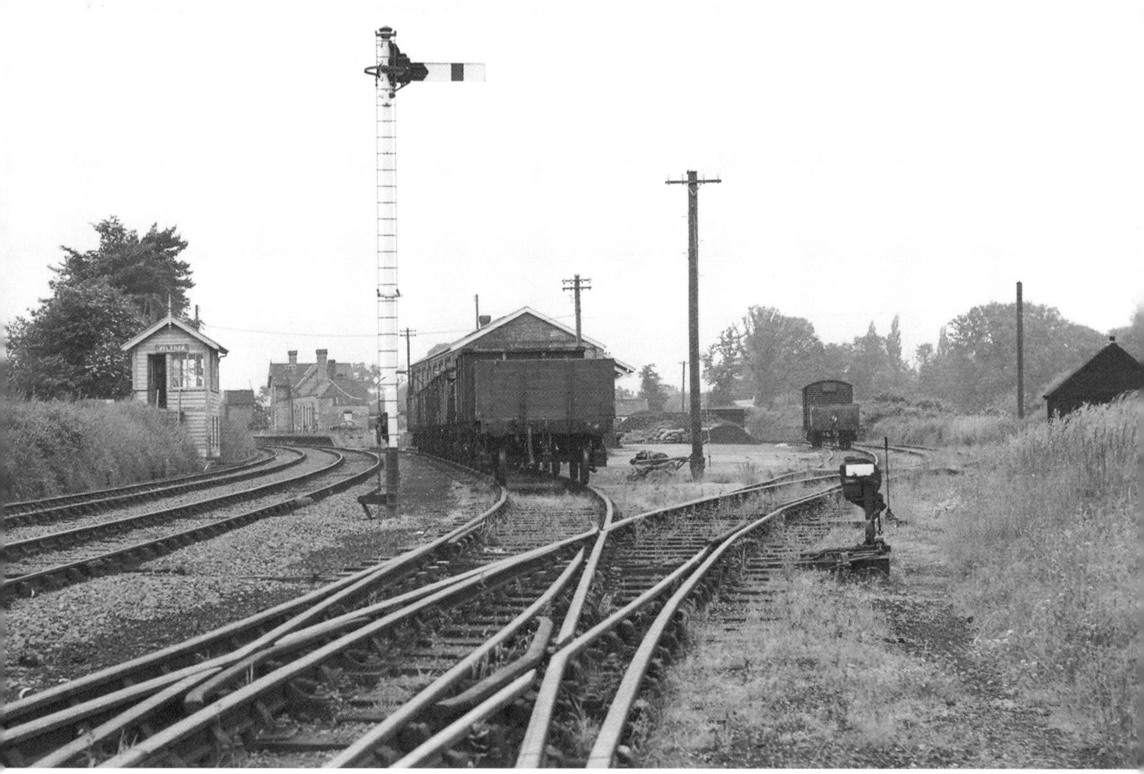

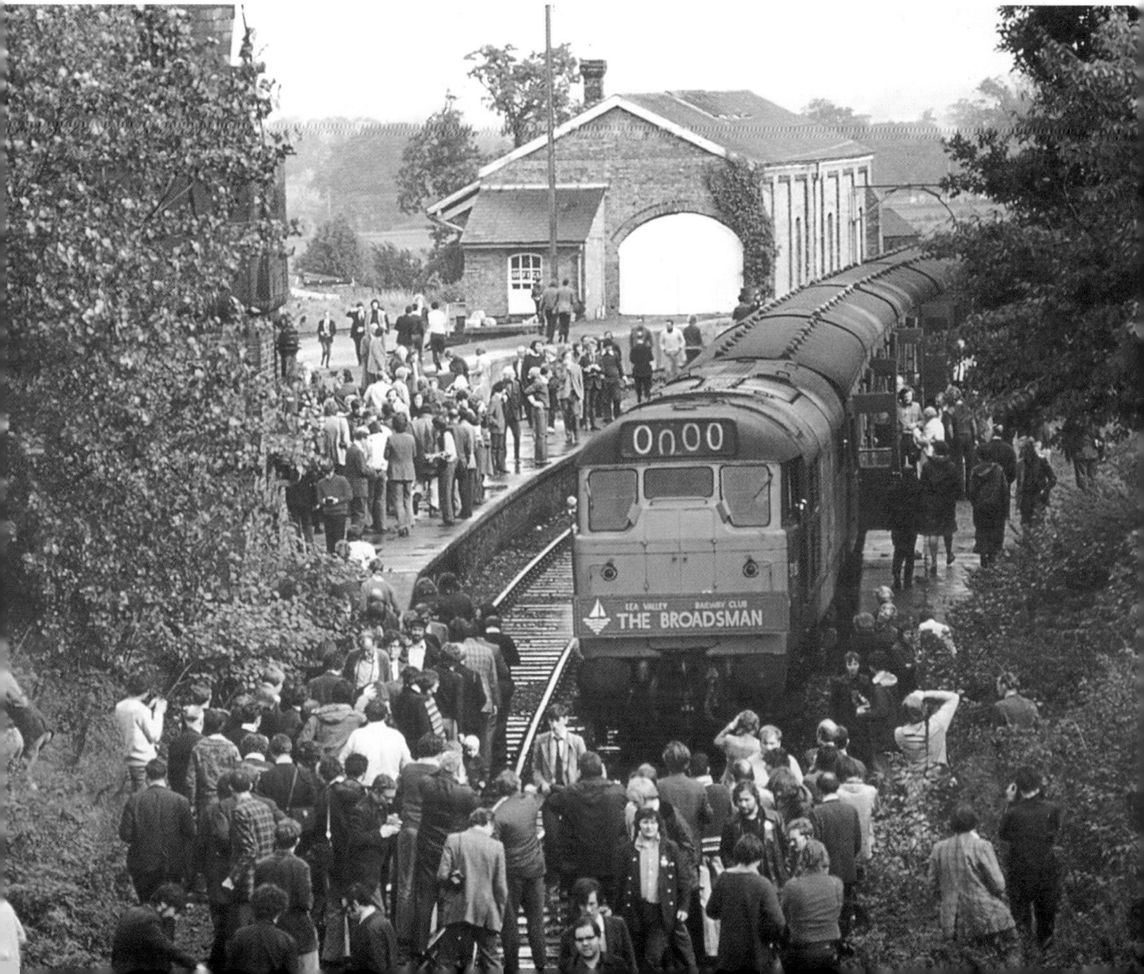
LEA VALLEY RAILWAY CLUB
THE BROADSMAN

78. The tracks were lifted during 1984, and the site was cleared by 1989 in readiness for the building of the Bure Valley Railway's station. This, together with redevelopment of the goods yard and surrounding area, quickly swept away all traces of the standard gauge infrastructure. However, the old goods shed remained for a year or two, and here it forms a backdrop to the turntable and RHDR loco *Samson* on 25th August 1990. (R.J.Adderson)

➔ 79. The redevelopment of the area is complete, as we survey a very busy scene on 13th September 2008. A new railway complex with car park, covered platforms, workshop facilities and substantial buildings incorporating a shop, refreshment room and tourist information office, now occupies the site. The bridge at the west end of the station was close to the mini roundabout in the bottom right hand corner of our picture. (M.Page)

➔ 80. With two Union Jacks fluttering from the buffer beam to mark the Diamond Jubilee of H.R.H.Queen Elizabeth II, no.7 *Spitfire* reverses to join its train, which is waiting underneath the overall roof on 2nd June 2012. The building to the right is the loco shed and workshop, which is fully equipped to deal with major overhaul work, as well as day to day maintenance. (R.J.Adderson)

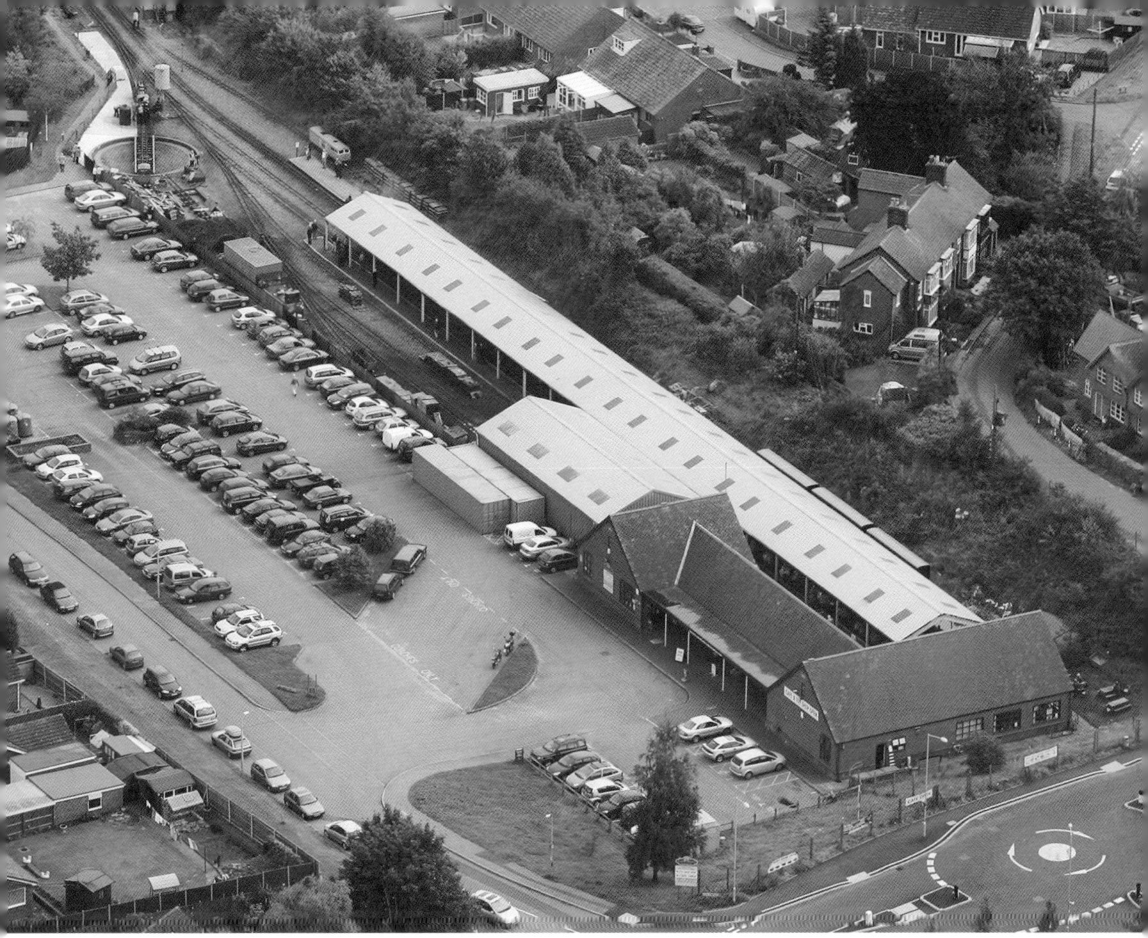

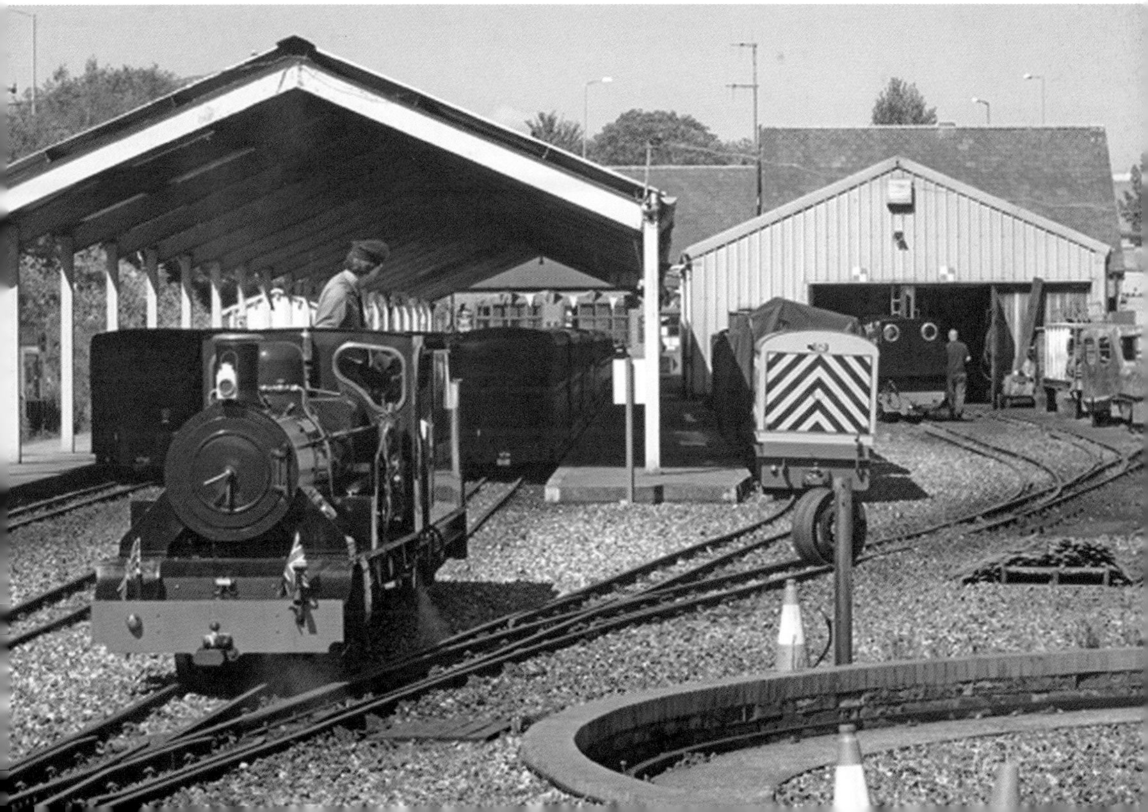

CAWSTON

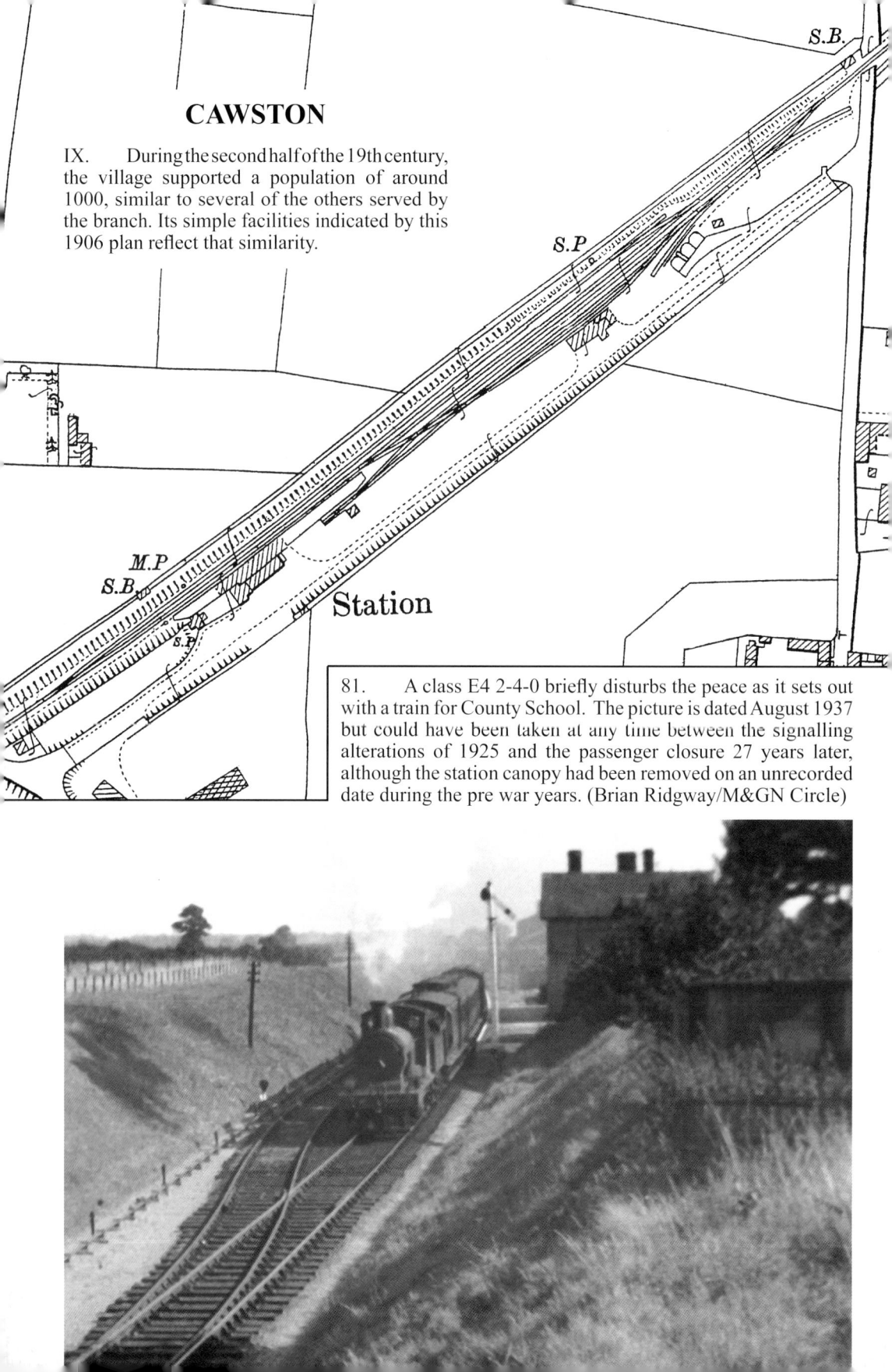

IX. During the second half of the 19th century, the village supported a population of around 1000, similar to several of the others served by the branch. Its simple facilities indicated by this 1906 plan reflect that similarity.

81. A class E4 2-4-0 briefly disturbs the peace as it sets out with a train for County School. The picture is dated August 1937 but could have been taken at any time between the signalling alterations of 1925 and the passenger closure 27 years later, although the station canopy had been removed on an unrecorded date during the pre war years. (Brian Ridgway/M&GN Circle)

82. A study of the map will reveal the two signal boxes (marked S.B.), which had been provided when the line was opened. Train operation was simplified in 1925 when the LNER replaced them with one signal box on the south side of the line adjacent to the level crossing. During the early years of World War II, two members of the staff pose for a photograph in the sunshine outside the new signal box. (Cawston Historical Society)

83. In contrasting weather conditions, this is the scene by the level crossing during the Arctic conditions of February 1947. The workmen have managed to clear a pathway along the road, but a good deal more hard labour will be needed before the level crossing gates are free to open. (Cawston Historical Society)

84. With the station in the distance, a grimy class D16/3 4-4-0 approaches the level crossing with five varied coaches and a van forming an eastbound train in July 1951. The lines to the left lead into the goods yard, which closed in October 1966, although some of the sidings survived for another decade and were occasionally used for storage purposes.
(E.Tuddenham/P.J.A.Bower/M&GN Circle)

85. Class J17 0-6-0 no. 65519 stands at the platform with a lightweight goods train returning from Reepham during the late 1950s. At this time, a daily goods train from Wensum Sidings at Norwich was sufficient to meet the demands of the branch stations. In 1959/60 it was scheduled to leave Wroxham at 9.27 am and arrive at Reepham just after noon. At 1.24 pm it set out back towards the main line, eventually arriving back at Wroxham at 4 pm. Six hours and thirty three minutes for a round trip of less than 31 miles allowed plenty of time for shunting the intermediate goods yards. (R.Harrison)

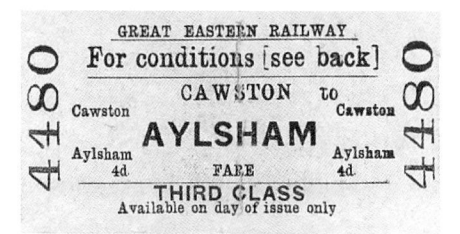

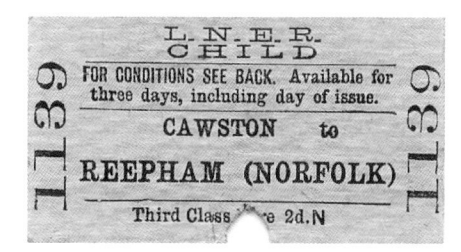

86. The Neptune track recording machine waits for the level crossing gates to be opened on 23rd June 1981. Although traffic was in terminal decline by the 1980s, maintenance and safety standards still had to be met. (G.L.Kenworthy)

87. Our final look at the station is, like our first, in shirt sleeves weather, as a DMU pauses at the well kept platform on 7th October 1972. This enthusiasts' special is returning from Lenwade to London and was the first passenger train on the line for almost exactly twelve years. The station building was still standing in 2012. (M.J.Wilson)

REEPHAM

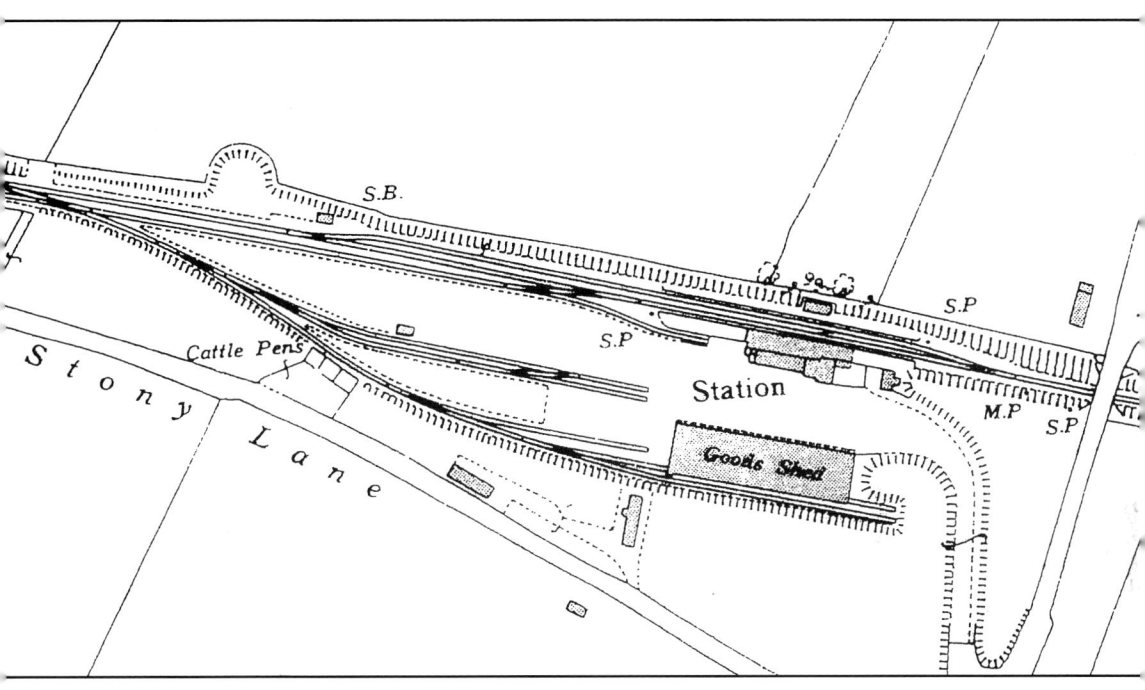

X. This 1938 edition shows the facilities serving this small market town close to their maximum. The station is located about ½ mile north of the town's market place. On the opposite side of the line from the cattle pens, the semi-circular feature marks the former location of a turntable. When the branch was first downgraded to the status of a light railway from Wroxham in 1957, the terminal point was stated to be approximately 300 yards west of this feature.

Local timetable 1930.

Wroxham, Aylsham and County School

WEEKDAYS

			Z		Z					Z		SX	SO
		a.m.	a.m.	a.m.	a.m.	p.m.	pm	p.m.	p.m.	p.m.	p.m.	p.m.	p.m.
Norwich (Thorpe)	dep.	6 21	9 10	9 43	1142	2 14	...	4 47	...	6 14	...	8 32	9 4
Whitlingham	,,	6 28	9 17	9 50	1150	2 21	...	4 54	...	6 21	...	8 39	9 11
Salhouse	,,	6 38	9 29	10 0	12 2	2 31	...	5 4	...	6 31	...	8 49	9 21
Wroxham	arr.	6 43	9 35	10 5	12 8	2 36	...	5 9	...	6 36	...	8 54	9 26
Cromer	dep.	...	8 09	10	...	1 0	...	3 45	...	5 28	...	7 29	7 29
Wroxham	arr.	...	8 26	9 47	...	1 34	...	4 19	...	6 6	...	8 8	8 8
Wroxham	dep.	6 44	9 36	10 7	12 9	2 38	...	5 11	...	6 41	...	8 56	9 28
Coltishall	,,	6 50	9 44	1013	1217	2 44	...	5 17	...	6 49	...	9 2	9 34
Buxton Lamas	,,	6 56	9 51	1019	1224	2 50	...	5 23	...	6 56	...	9 8	9 40
Aylsham	,,	7 5	9 58	1028	1234	2 58	...	5 34	...	7 5	...	9 16	9 48
Cawston	,,	7 14	—	1037	1244	3 7	...	5 43	...	7 15	...	9 25	9 57
Reepham	,,	7 21	...	1042	1250	3 12	...	5 48	...	7 21	...	9 30	10 2
Foulsham	,,	7 30	...	1051	1 0	3 21	...	5 57	...	7 35	...	9 39	1011
County School	arr.	7 38	...	1059	1 8	3 29	...	6 5	...	7 43	...	9 47	1019

    s   On Saturdays arrives Wymondham 7.31 and Norwich (Thorpe) 7.55 p.m.
    j   On Saturdays leaves County School 4.59 and arrives Fakenham 5.14 and
            Wells-on-Sea 5.37 p.m.
    Z   Steam Rail Car.   SX   Saturdays excepted.   SO   Saturdays only.   a Weds. only

88. Here we have another of the platform views so beloved by photographers in the early years of the twentieth century, and as with the picture at Coltishall, the station master's daughter has been allowed to join the group of railwaymen. The branch stations, although at first glance very similar, all had detail differences, and here the awnings were supported by iron stanchions, which were a lot more slender and stylish than the functional wooden props we have seen at the stations further east. (Lens of Sutton coll.)

➜ 89. It is a busy time for the staff, as two passenger trains cross in the loop. The picture is taken from a postcard bearing a July 1914 postmark, so it is likely that the trains are the 2.09 pm Wroxham to County School and the 2.30 pm County School to Wroxham, as these were the only two passenger trains booked to pass here in the 1913 timetable.
(P.Standley coll.)

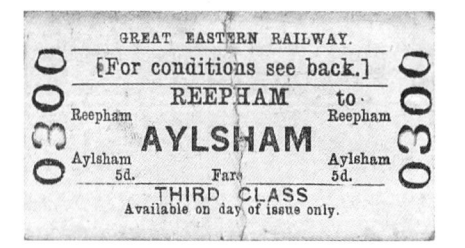

➜ 90. Class F6 2-4-2T no. 67224 sets out with the 2.33 pm train from Wroxham to Dereham on 12th September 1951. This train was scheduled to leave Reepham at 3.09 pm and to arrive at its destination 30 minutes later. The leading vehicle is a full brake, used for carrying parcels and packages. It would appear that this traffic was still heavy right up to the passenger closure, as several trains of the era included this type of vehicle.
(E.Tuddenham/P.J.A.Bower/M&GN Circle)

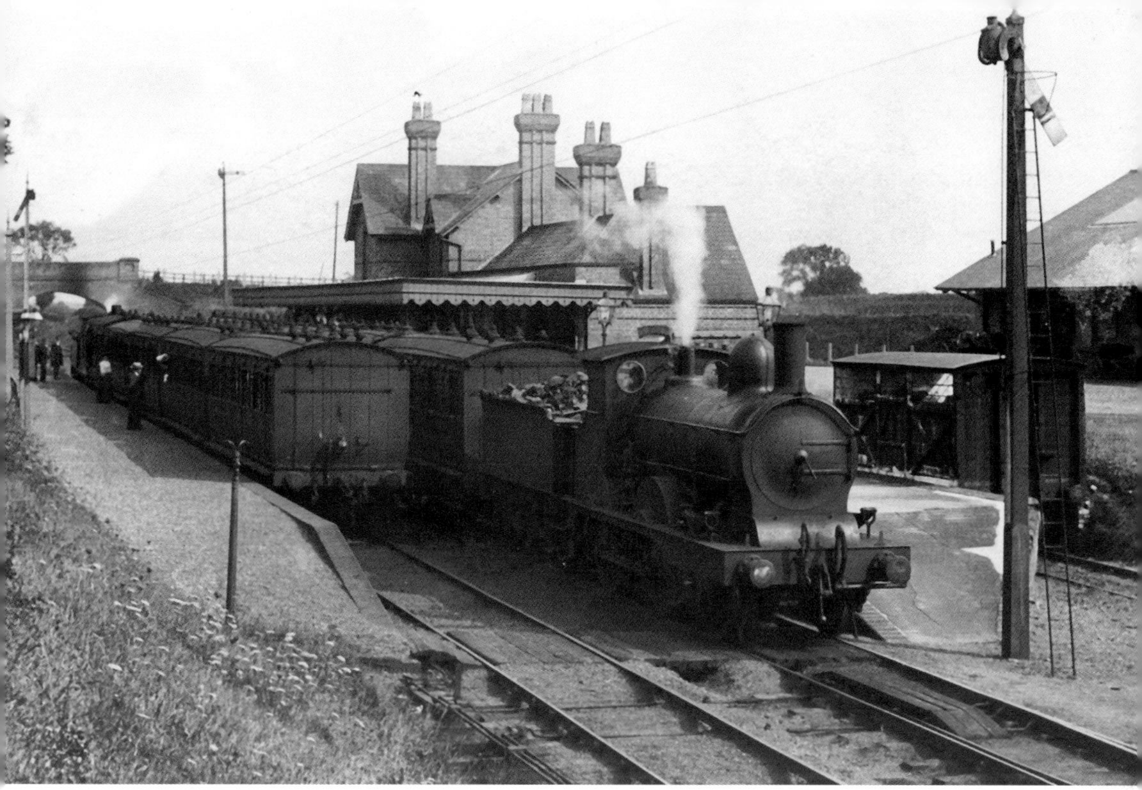

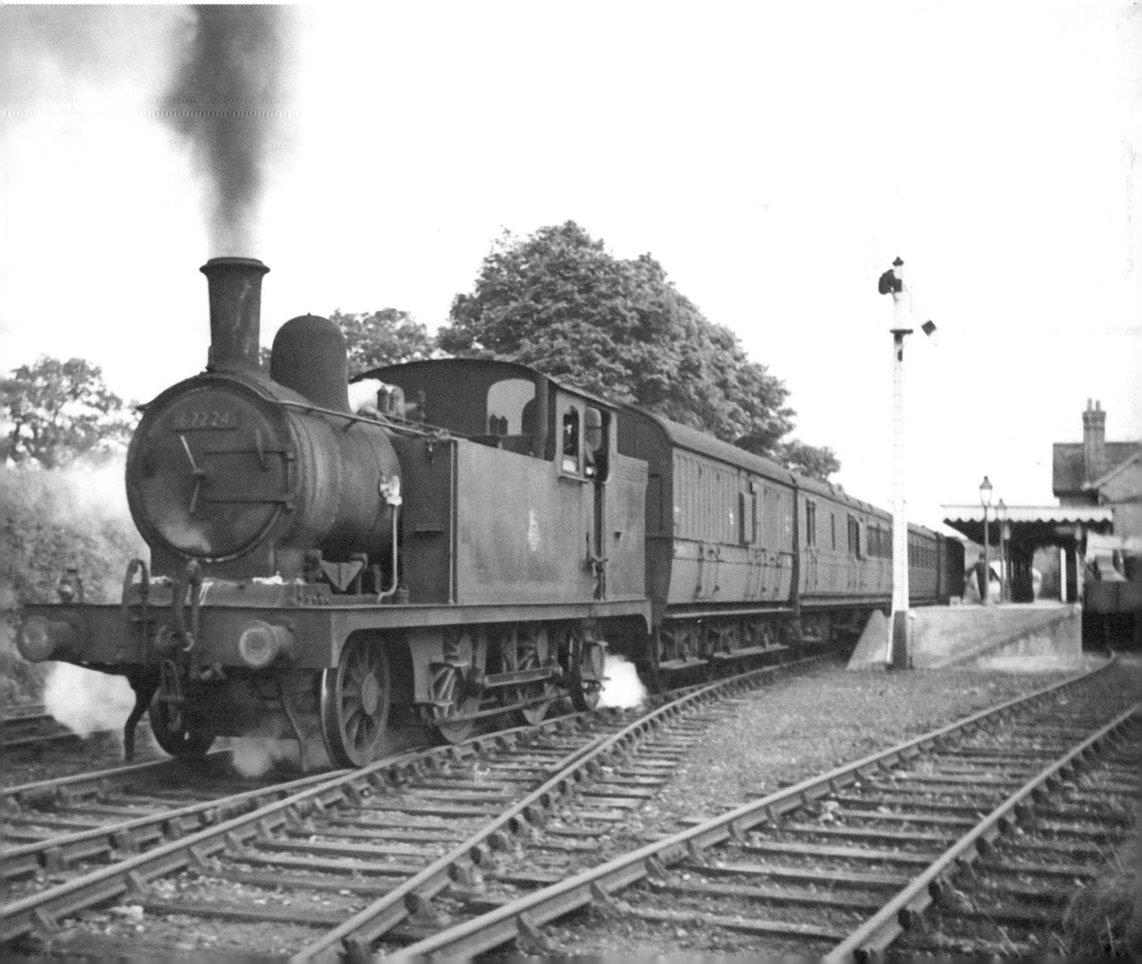

91. Class J17 0-6-0 no. 65566 occupies itself with some wagons at the east end of the station on 22nd May 1956. Now that passenger trains no longer run, the platforms are looking somewhat neglected, and the signals will be dismantled by the end of the year. The lettering on the wall of the building beyond the railway proclaims it to be Collers Drying Plant. R Coller and Son was a prominent local business, described as "Coal, corn, cake and salt merchants" in 1900, and nearby Collers Way perpetuated the name into the 21st century. (P.Worship/M&GN Circle)

➜ 92. No.65566 has again been rostered to work the branch goods train, and has reached the most southerly of the yard sidings on Christmas Eve 1956. The shunter jogs alongside, equipped to couple or uncouple wagons with one deft flick of his shunting pole. His job was a strenuous one, and at times a risky one, but tomorrow he'll be able to relax over his Christmas dinner. (P.Worship/ M&GN Circle)

➜ 93. A weed killing train disturbs the afternoon peace as it runs into the station on Sunday 24th April 1960. Train workings over the branch on the Sabbath were very rare indeed. The locomotive, 4MT 2-6-0 no. 43160, had been based at Norwich Thorpe shed for the previous 14 months, but still carries a 32F shed plate as a reminder of its previous allocation to Yarmouth Beach depot. (P.Worship/M&GN Circle)

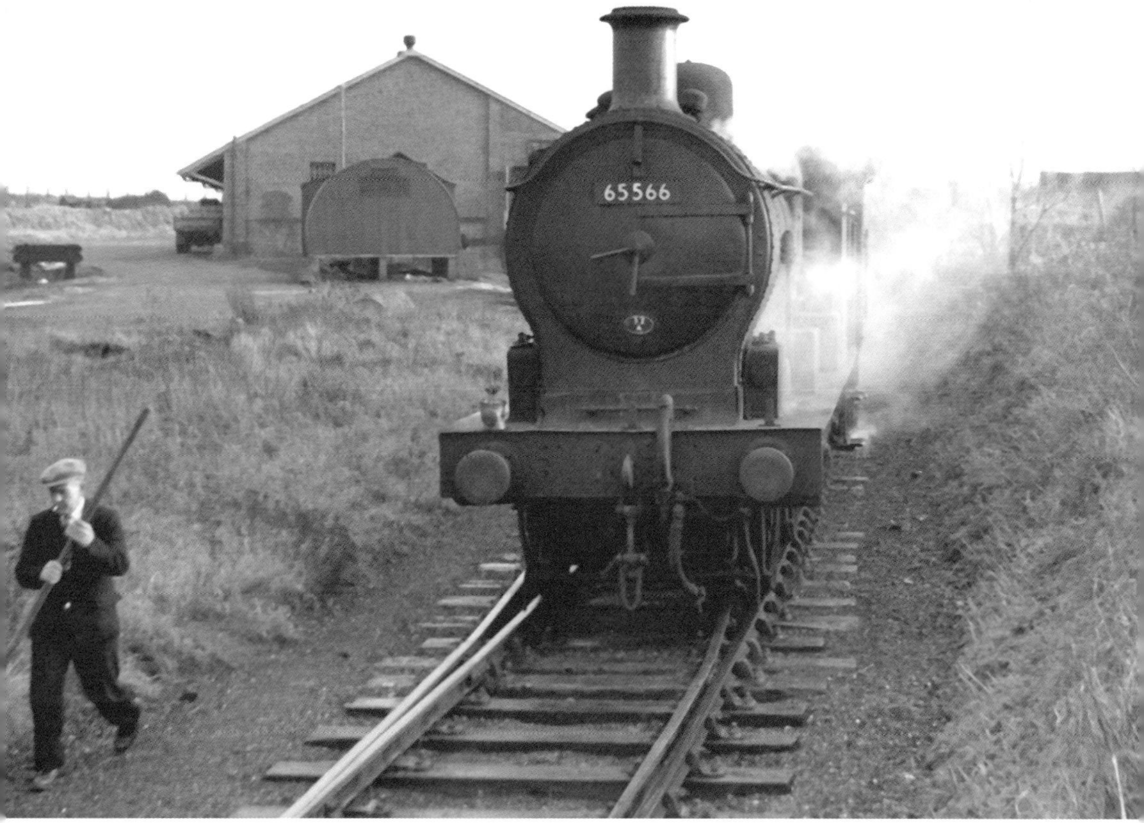
65566

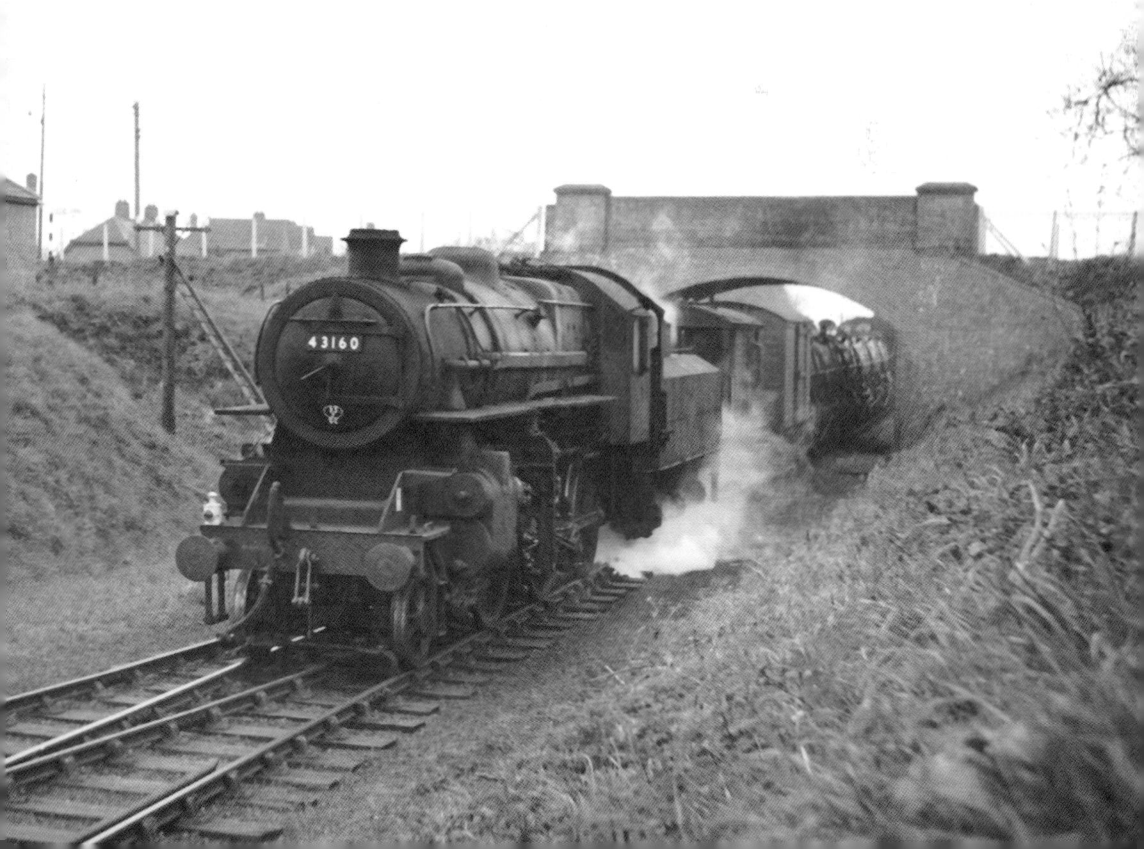
43160

94. The station master's son was able to photograph another unusual sight a few days later, on 7th May 1960, when diesel shunter no D2036 formed part of the engineering train involved in relaying the line westwards. Roughly patched areas on the surface of the platform indicate where the awning supports had been uprooted. (P.Worship/M&GN Circle)

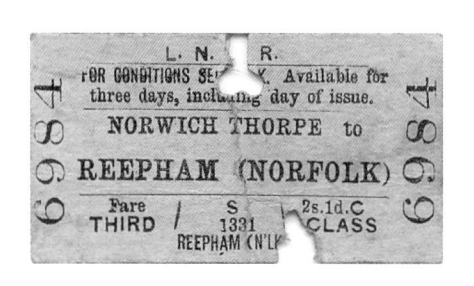

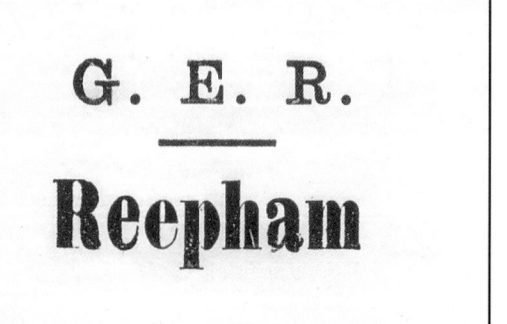

95. Passing the cabin and 4-lever ground frame which had replaced the signal box some six months earlier, no. D8202 approaches the station with an eastbound goods train on 15th March 1961. The concrete beams had originated at Lenwade, on the Norwich branch of the M&GN, and the train has reached the East Norfolk line by means of the new Themelthorpe curve. (P. Worship/ M&GN Circle)

96. In its day, the yard was busy with a variety of goods traffic, including cattle, horses, fertiliser, coal and sugar beet, and the 1½ ton crane played a valuable role in dealing with this. The design was fairly basic, but it was still to be seen on 12th March 1964. (J. Watling)

97.　We are looking eastwards from the entrance to the goods sidings on 17th July 1966, a picture which emphasises the extent of the land which the yard occupied. The substantial granary, sometimes described as "goods shed" is prominent to the right of the picture, and over the years the facilities were shared by local businesses dealing in coal, grain and animal feedstuffs.
(Railway Record of the British Isles/G.L.Pring)

➜　98. Goods traffic to the yard lingered on into the 1970s, but freight trains continued to pass through the platforms until the early 1980s. The majority of these, conveying massive concrete products from the factory at Lenwade, were a far cry from the leisurely pick up goods trains of the steam age. One such train, double headed by a pair of Brush type 2 diesels, heads east in the Spring sunshine in April 1969. (G.H.Smith)

➜　99. In 2012, the station building was in use as a gift shop and tea room, whilst the goods shed was serving as a pine furniture warehouse. Externally, neither had changed much when this picture was taken on 19th April, as Marriott's Way footpath makes its way through the platforms. The first edition Ordnance Survey map of 1879/86 shows the turntable connected to the loop by a trailing connection running in front of the signal box, but it could only ever have been of limited use, and was very short lived. However, the site of the installation was still obvious on this wet April afternoon, as the photographer found the railway boundary fence curving outwards in a semi circle to accommodate it, just as it did when the map was surveyed some 130 years earlier.
(R.J.Adderson)

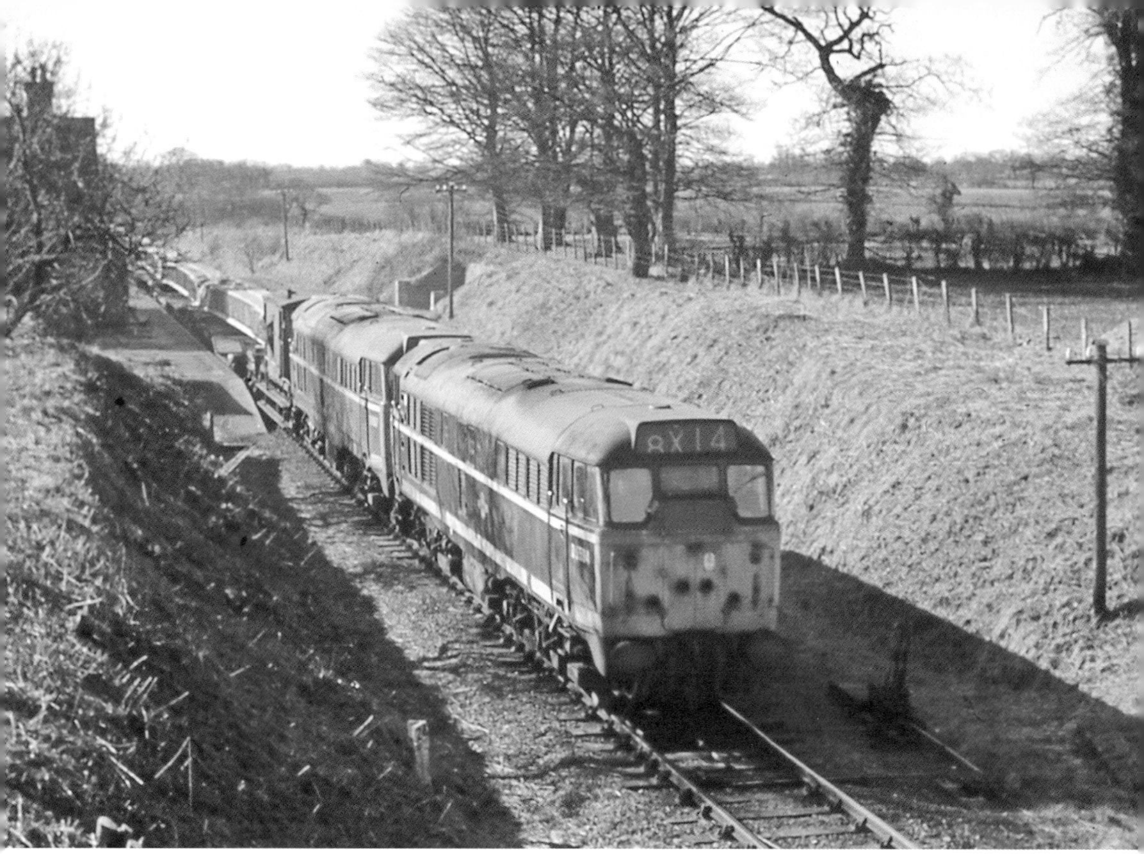
8X14

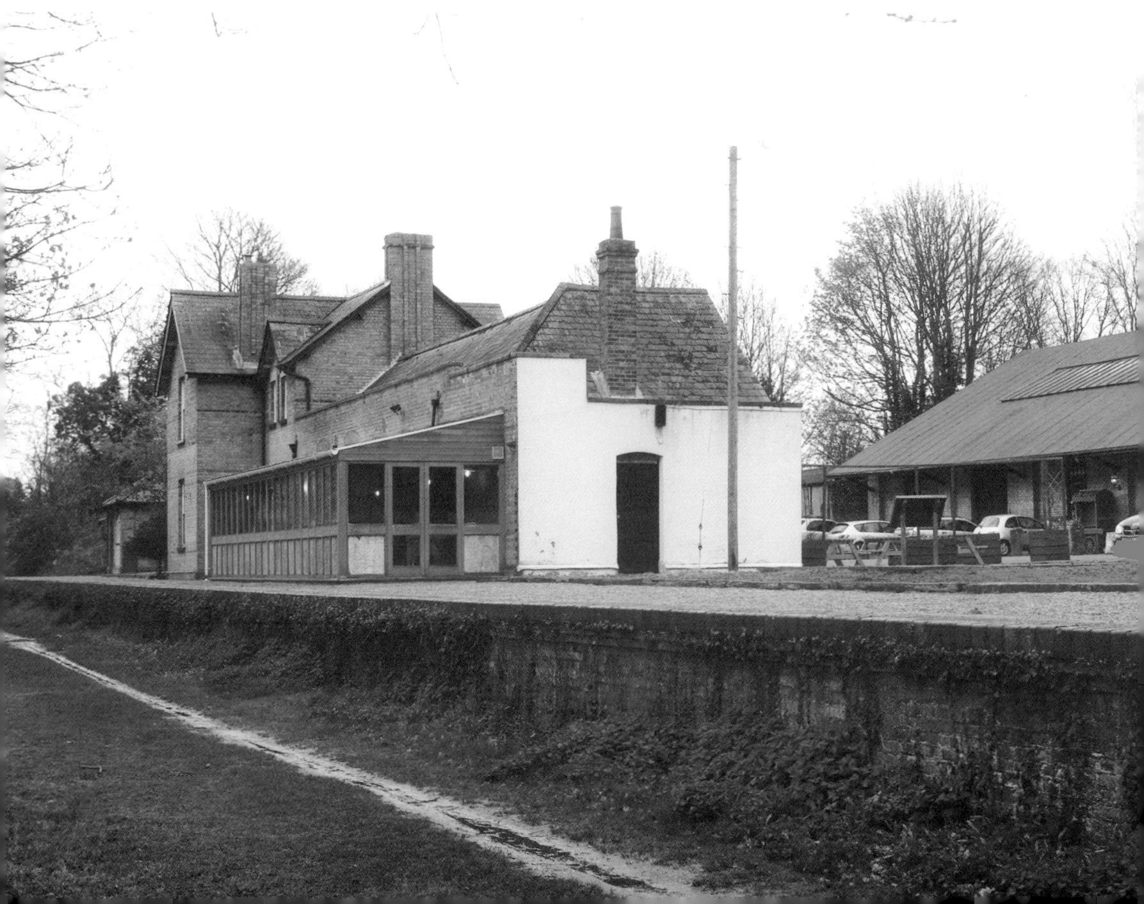

WEST OF REEPHAM

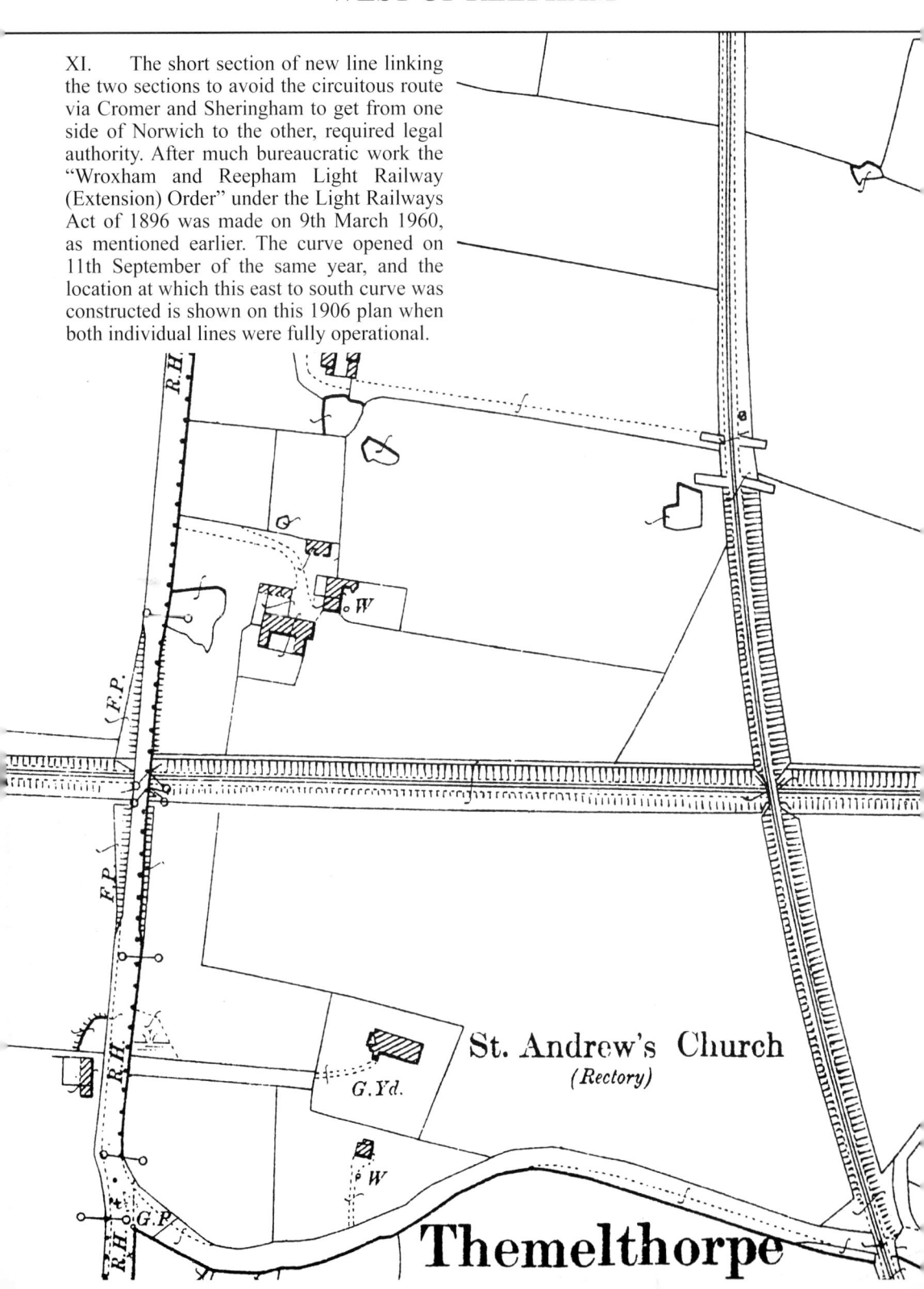

XI. The short section of new line linking the two sections to avoid the circuitous route via Cromer and Sheringham to get from one side of Norwich to the other, required legal authority. After much bureaucratic work the "Wroxham and Reepham Light Railway (Extension) Order" under the Light Railways Act of 1896 was made on 9th March 1960, as mentioned earlier. The curve opened on 11th September of the same year, and the location at which this east to south curve was constructed is shown on this 1906 plan when both individual lines were fully operational.

St. Andrew's Church
(Rectory)

G.Yd.

Themelthorpe

100. The line ceased to be a through route in February 1955 following total closure of the section between Reepham and Foulsham, although part of it was used for a while to store surplus wagons. Class J19 0-6-0 no.64644 is engaged on track lifting duties on the abandoned section on 20th March 1957. There was nothing subtle about the operation; successive track panels were simply unbolted, roped to the coupling hook of the locomotive and then dragged away along the line for disposal. (P.Worship/ M&GN Circle)

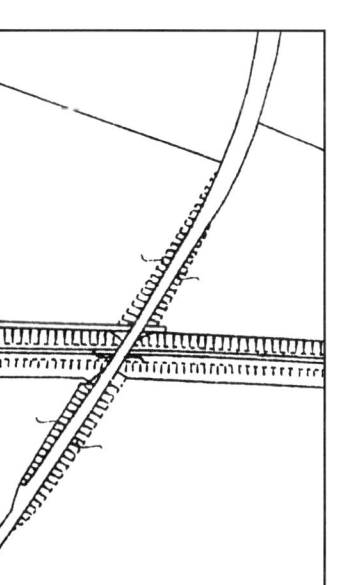

101. After the tracks were lifted, the branch from Wroxham terminated at buffer stops just to the west of Reepham station. This was the end of the line on 31st August 1957, a situation which proved to be unexpectedly short lived. (R.Harrison)

102. Few people could have foretold that within three years a track laying gang would be at work, busily relaying the line. Here a road crane has lifted a length of track from the railway wagon, prior to moving forward to lay it carefully in place on the ballast. Once this panel has been connected, the 0-6-0 diesel shunter will propel the wagon forward over the newly-laid track, and the procedure will start all over again. Pettywell Road bridge, a mile and a half or so west of Reepham station, is in the distance. (E.Tuddenham/P.J.A.Bower/M&GN Circle)

103. The line towards Foulsham was reinstated for some 2½ miles to a point close to the village of Themelthorpe. From here a completely new stretch of railway was built, swinging sharply southwards and climbing to join up with the former M&GN branch from Norwich City to Melton Constable. This is the start of the new curve during the Summer of 1960, with the trackbed of the line to Foulsham carrying straight on under the two bridges, the second one of which carried the M&GN line. (NRS Archive)

104. No.31268 observes the 10 mph speed limit as it heads an empty stock train round the sharply curved 518 yard stretch of new railway on 18th April 1980. The photographer is standing on a farm track which was once the M&GN line, with his back to the bridge, and the level crossing gatehouse is to the right of the coaches. Earlier in the day the coaches had formed a school special from Aylsham to Ely and back, and had then been hauled to Lenwade to enable the engine to run round, as there was no longer a loop anywhere else on the line. (R.J.Adderson)

105. In 2012 the course of the railway as it was from 1960 onwards forms part of a long distance footpath, Marriott's Way, and as such can be traced quite easily between Aylsham and the outskirts of Norwich. By contrast, the M&GN line northwards to Melton Constable was abandoned once the new curve was opened, while the trackbed westwards to Foulsham was also left to merge gradually into the landscape. A few traces of these lines survived though; here we are looking westwards, past the abutments of the M&GN bridge at Themelthorpe to the GER cutting beyond. (S.McNae)

FOULSHAM

106. During Great Eastern days a class T26 2-4-0 stands at the platform, heading west with a train formed of 6 wheel coaches. Engines of this class, by then known as class E4, were still active on the line on the final day of passenger services. The yard crane, similar to the one we have seen at Reepham, is prominent to the left of the picture, while the signal box by the level crossing is one of the two originally provided here, one at each end of the station. (A.R.Taylor coll.)

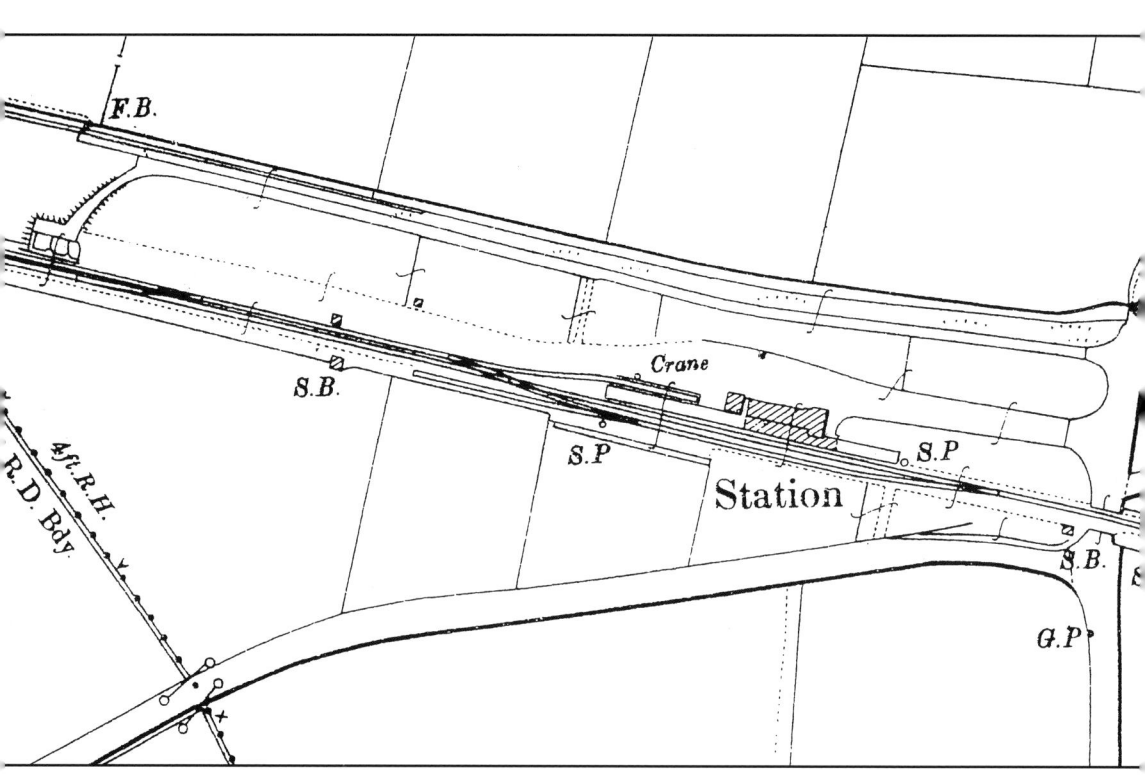

XII. The village to the north of the station had been almost completely destroyed by fire in 1770, but, by the time the railway was proposed, both village and population had fully recovered. However by the time of this 1939 plan, the number of residents was once again in decline.

1880 letter sent during construction of branch.

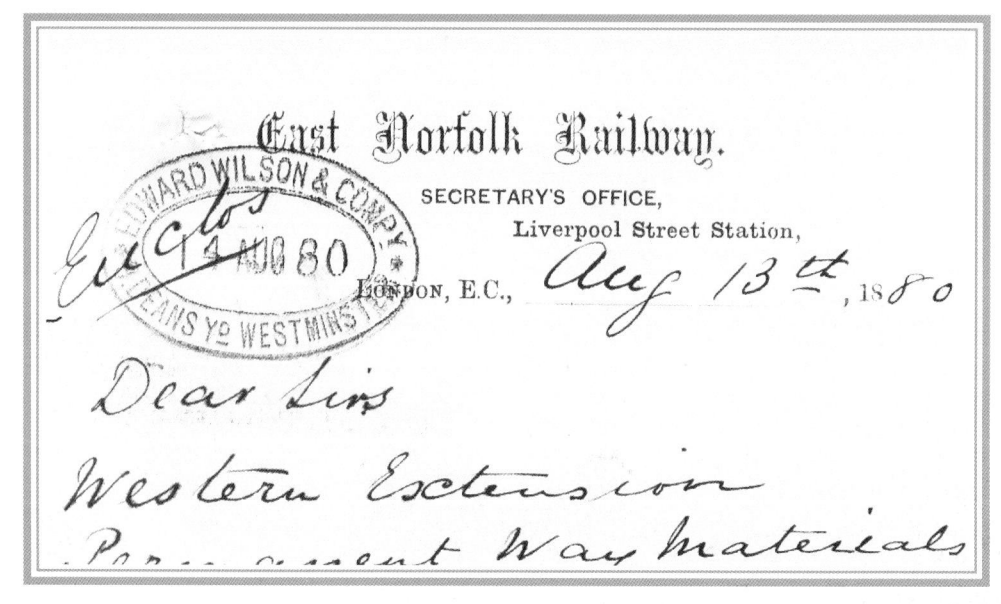

East Norfolk Railway.

SECRETARY'S OFFICE,
Liverpool Street Station,
LONDON, E.C., Aug 13th, 1880

Dear Sirs

Western Extension
Permanent Way Materials

107. Looking in the other direction at much the same time, we can see the western signal box beyond the signal post, opposite the wagons in the goods yard. Both signal boxes were abolished in 1925, and were replaced by the structure which appears in later pictures. The station was provided with a loop, but only one platform, so two passenger trains could not pass here. (P.Standley coll.)

108. Looking across the vegetable garden, we are able to obtain a good idea of the extent of the station and canopy. We have already commented on some of the differences between the station buildings along the line, and another one is apparent here. Together with Cawston, this is one of the two locations where the two storey residential section was to be found to the right of the public buildings when viewed from the platform. This picture also dates from Great Eastern days. (A.R.Taylor coll.)

109. It's washday at Foulsham during the early Summer of 1951, and the station master's wife is no doubt hoping that passing enginemen will keep their smoke emissions to a minimum. With just over a year of passenger services left, the station building is looking somewhat bare following the removal of the canopy and decorative timber work on the gable.
(Stations U.K)

➜ 110. Moving forward in time to February 1957, we find that the line eastwards towards Reepham has recently been lifted after some two years of disuse. For the moment, the signals and level crossing gates are still in place, guarding an empty trackbed.
(P.Worship/M&GN Circle)

➜ 111. Class J19 0-6-0 no. 64674 is ready to depart with a goods train on a Winter's day in the late 1950s. Most of the load is made up of open wagons piled high with sugar beet bound for one of Norfolk's processing factories. This traffic brought much needed revenue to many small country goods yards, but it was seasonal, lasting for no more than three months of the year. Unusually, the lever frame faced the rear of the signal box.
(I.C.Allen/Transport Treasury)

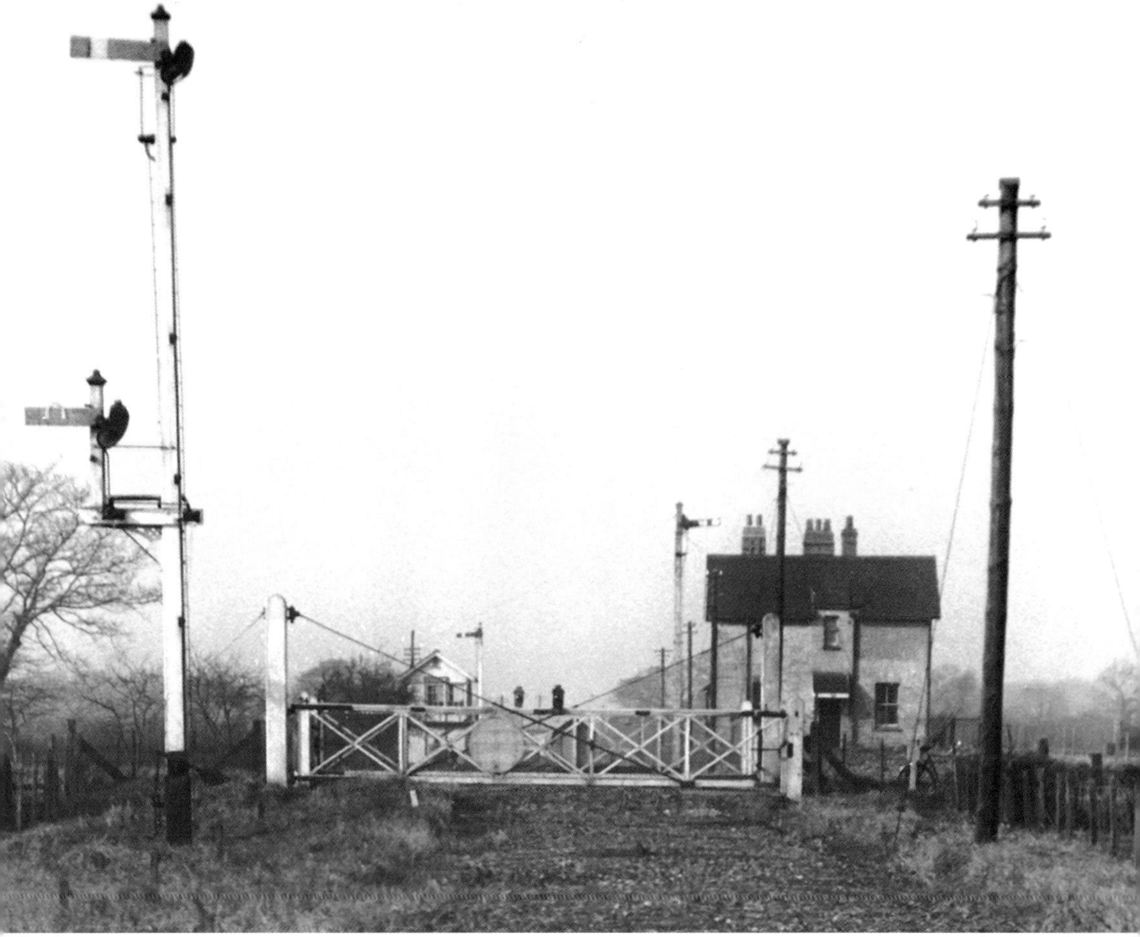

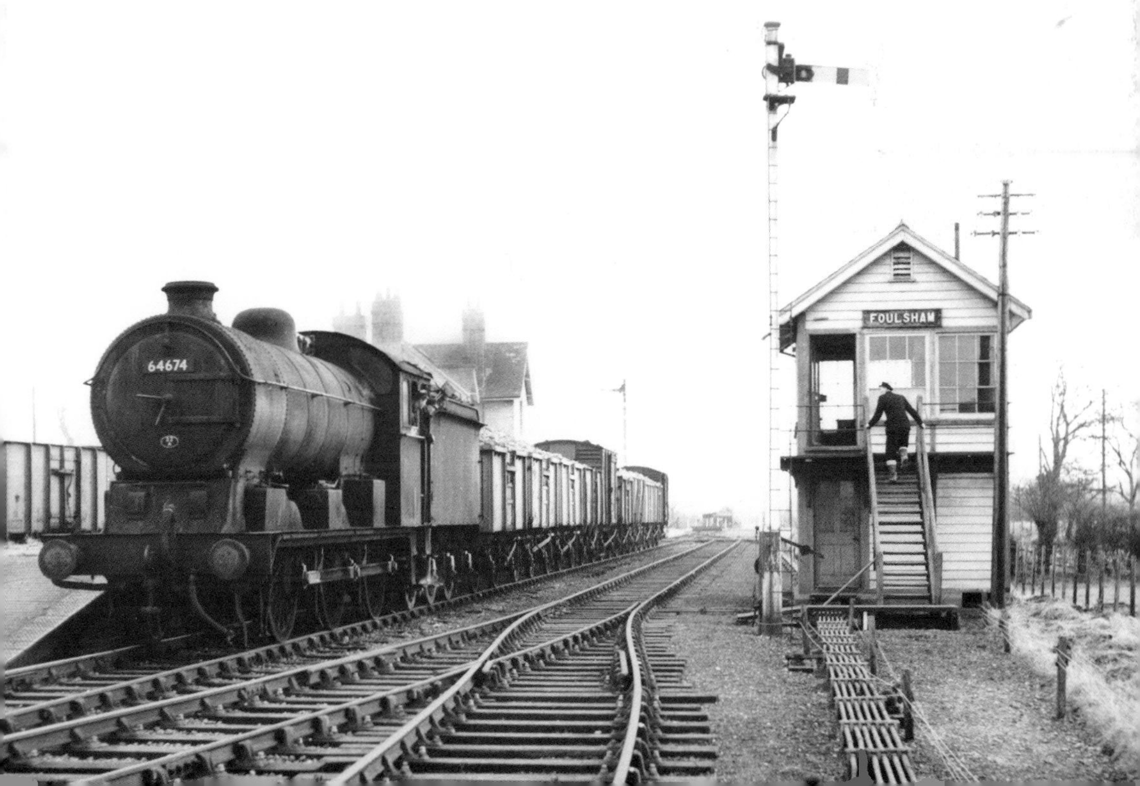
64674
FOULSHAM

112. On 31st March 1962, the station was visited by a railtour which ran to mark the end of steam traction on the former Great Eastern system. Class J17 0-6-0 no. 65567 stands at the platform with this train, as crowds of enthusiasts make what is probably their first and only visit to the station. The train was hauled from London and back by a Britannia pacific, while the J17 gave participants a roundabout tour of some of the branch lines in the area, all of which would lose their passenger services by the end of the decade. (A.Swain/Transport Treasury)

113. Now we move forward to October 1964, when the branch goods train ran only twice a week, on Mondays and Thursdays. It was scheduled to arrive from Dereham at 12.49 pm and to head back at 1.18 pm. By this time, the whole area is looking sadly neglected and the line will close completely at the end of the month. The tracks were soon removed, but the station building survived in 2012. (R.Powell)

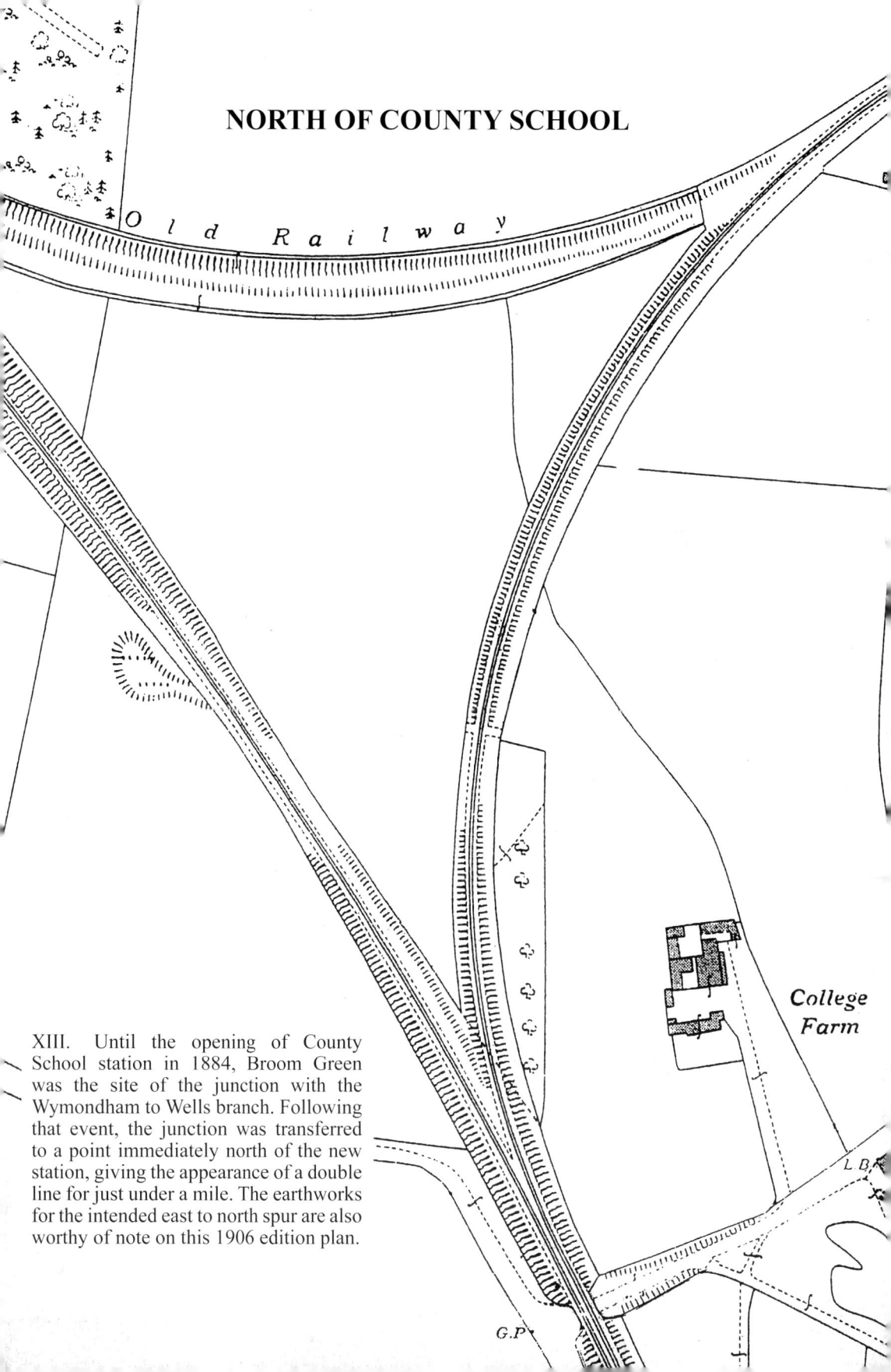

NORTH OF COUNTY SCHOOL

Old Railway

College Farm

G.P

XIII. Until the opening of County School station in 1884, Broom Green was the site of the junction with the Wymondham to Wells branch. Following that event, the junction was transferred to a point immediately north of the new station, giving the appearance of a double line for just under a mile. The earthworks for the intended east to north spur are also worthy of note on this 1906 edition plan.

114. A passenger train, hauled by a grubby class E4 2-4-0, curves away from the Wells line and heads east along the branch towards Foulsham during the very early 1950s. Such trains were undoubtedly full of character, but by now all the communities they served enjoyed direct bus services to Norwich, and the traffic potential on this east to west route must have been limited. Following the withdrawal of passenger trains, Eastern Counties Omnibus Company provided Service 70 running between Dereham and Wroxham as a direct replacement, but by the early 1960s this no longer ran east of Aylsham and it disappeared completely from the timetables within a few years. (I.C.Allen/Transport Treasury)

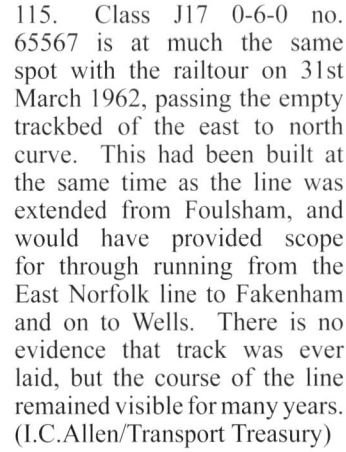

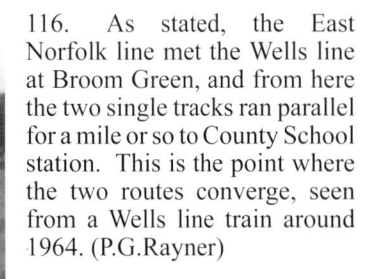

115. Class J17 0-6-0 no. 65567 is at much the same spot with the railtour on 31st March 1962, passing the empty trackbed of the east to north curve. This had been built at the same time as the line was extended from Foulsham, and would have provided scope for through running from the East Norfolk line to Fakenham and on to Wells. There is no evidence that track was ever laid, but the course of the line remained visible for many years. (I.C.Allen/Transport Treasury)

116. As stated, the East Norfolk line met the Wells line at Broom Green, and from here the two single tracks ran parallel for a mile or so to County School station. This is the point where the two routes converge, seen from a Wells line train around 1964. (P.G.Rayner)

COUNTY SCHOOL

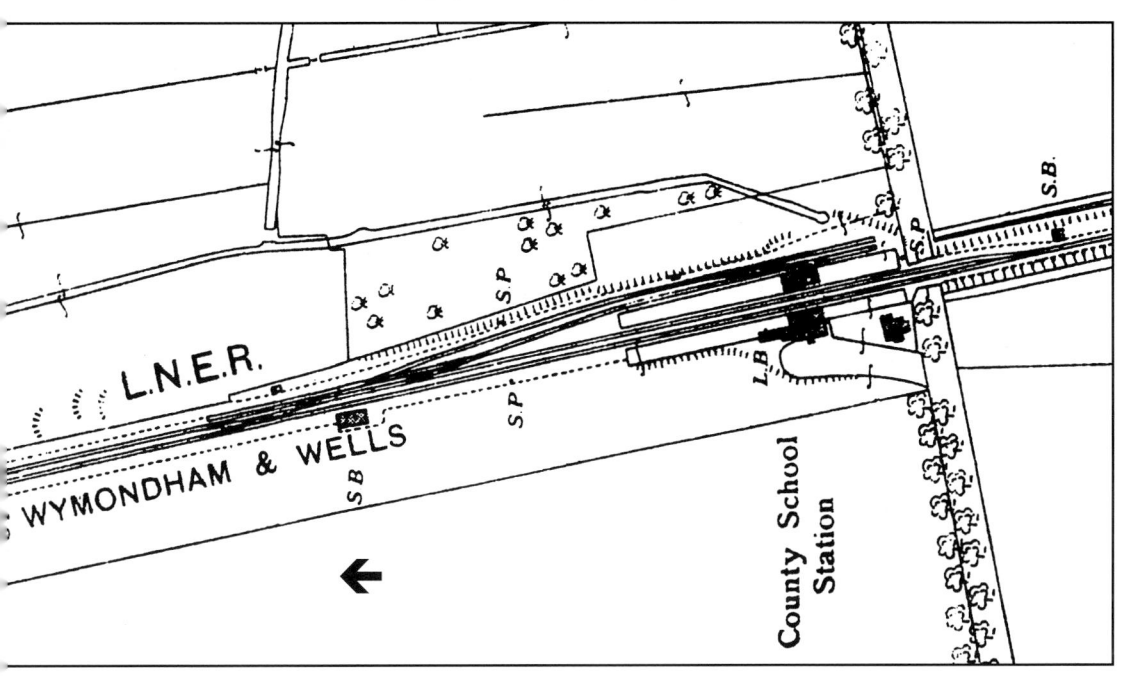

XIV. The school after which the station was named was a public school, developed in the late 1870s. Its founder, Joseph Brereton, persuaded the Great Eastern Railway to provide railway access and the station opened on 1st March 1884. The opportunity was taken to terminate most branch services here instead of running through to Dereham, although this practice was relatively short-lived. After a varied history, the school closed in 1953, shortly after closure of the branch from Wroxham, but the station survived until closure of the Dereham to Wells service on 5th October 1964. The plan is the 1939 edition.

117. Enamel signs proliferate, as we look southwards during the late 1930s. We are standing on the island platform, the left hand face of which was used by trains terminating here. This was little used in later years, when most trains worked through to Dereham. (Stations UK)

118. Class D16/3 4-4-0 no.62593 runs into the station with a train from Wells on 23rd August 1952. It is passing an informative running in board, which not only lists some of the destinations which can be reached by changing here, but perpetuates the name of the company which had promoted the line some 75 years earlier. Just three weeks later, the sign would become redundant with the withdrawal of passenger services over the Wroxham line, and by sheer coincidence, it was no.62593 which hauled the very last train. (R.J.Adderson coll.)

→ 119. After running parallel from Broom Green, the single tracks of the Wells and East Norfolk lines were eventually connected just north of the station, where a scissors crossover neatly catered for all the likely train movements at this point. We are looking towards the station from the dizzy heights of a signal post on 10th October 1964, a week after the last passenger trains ran to Wells, and three weeks before the Foulsham line was closed entirely. (J.Watling)

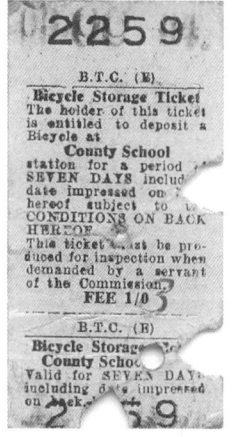

→ 120. Following the withdrawal of passenger trains on the Wells line, occasional goods trains continued to pass through the increasingly overgrown platforms until the early 1980s. Here no. D5663 makes its way north with the daily goods train for Fakenham on 4th July 1968. In later years the station became the site of a short lived preservation scheme, but by 2012 had settled into a far more tranquil existence, delightfully restored and serving as a tea room. There is still the possibility that it will one day be linked with the private Mid Norfolk Railway, as it extends north from Dereham. Time will tell….. (Railway Record of the British Isles/G.L.Pring)

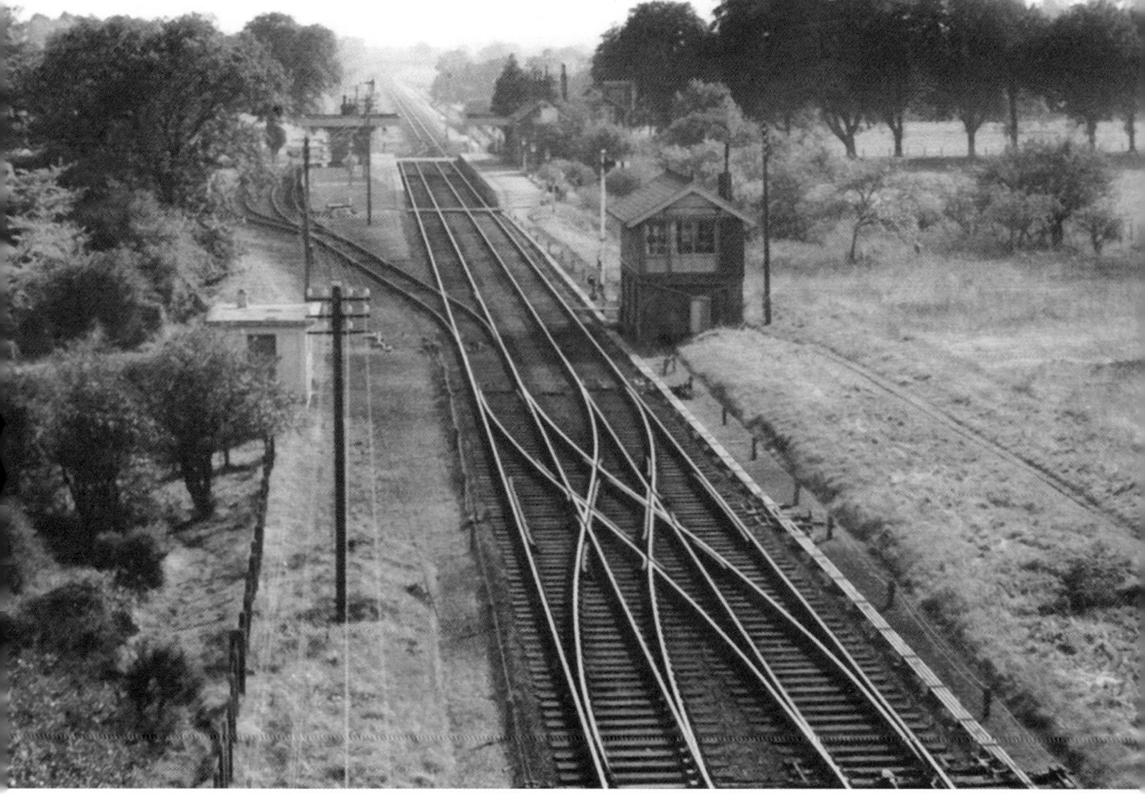

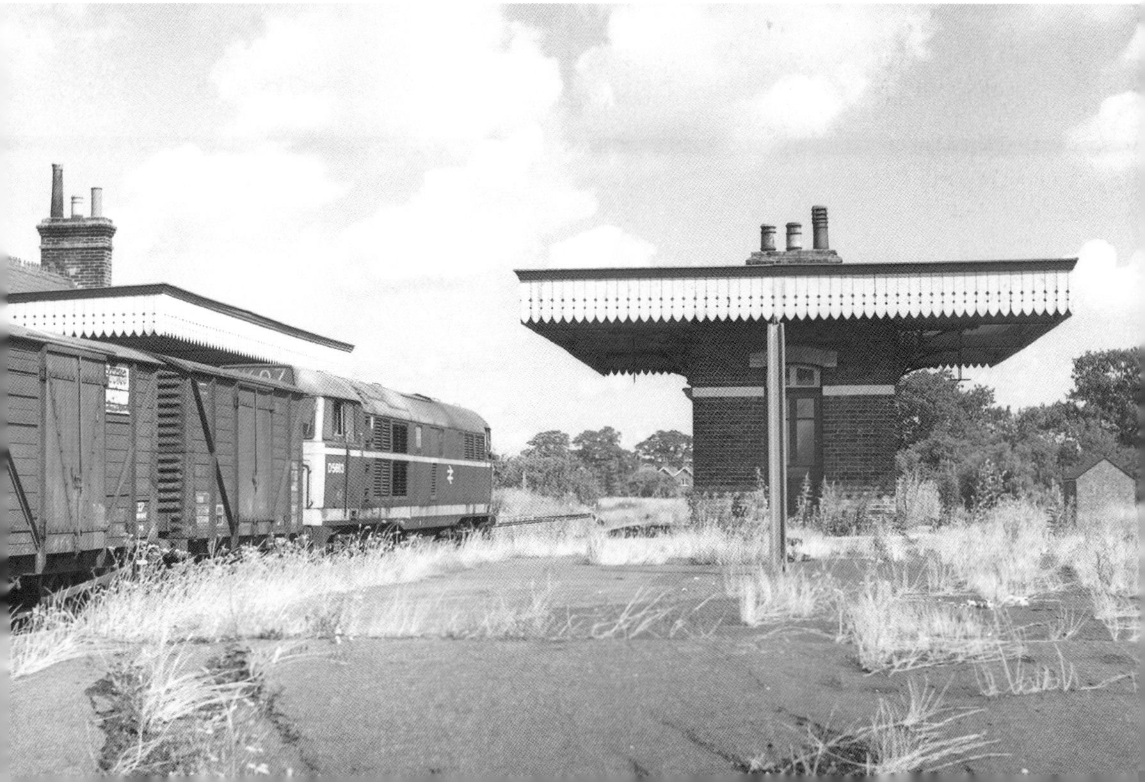

MP Middleton Press
EVOLVING THE ULTIMATE RAIL ENCYCLOPEDIA

Easebourne Lane, Midhurst, West Sussex.
GU29 9AZ   Tel:01730 813169
www.middletonpress.co.uk   email:info@middletonpress.co.uk
A-978 0 906520   B- 978 1 873793   C- 978 1 901706   D-978 1 904474
E - 978 1 906008   F - 978 1 908174

All titles listed below were in print at time of publication - please check current availability by looking at our website - www.middletonpress.co.uk or by requesting a Brochure which includes our LATEST RAILWAY TITLES also our TRAMWAY, TROLLEYBUS, MILITARY and COASTAL series

A
Abergavenny to Merthyr C 91 8
Abertillery & Ebbw Vale Lines D 84 5
Aberystwyth to Carmarthen E 90 1
Allhallows - Branch Line to A 62 8
Alton - Branch Lines to A 11 6
Andover to Southampton A 82 6
Ascot - Branch Lines around A 64 2
Ashburton - Branch Line to B 95 4
Ashford - Steam to Eurostar B 67 1
Ashford to Dover A 48 2
Austrian Narrow Gauge D 04 3
Avonmouth - BL around D 42 5
Aylesbury to Rugby D 91 3

B
Baker Street to Uxbridge D 90 6
Bala to Llandudno E 87 1
Banbury to Birmingham D 27 2
Banbury to Cheltenham E 63 5
Bangor to Holyhead F 01 7
Bangor to Portmadoc E 72 7
Barking to Southend C 80 2
Barmouth to Pwllheli E 53 6
Barry - Branch Lines around D 50 0
Bartlow - Branch Lines to F 27 7
Bath Green Park to Bristol C 36 9
Bath to Evercreech Junction A 60 4
Beamish 40 years on rails E94 9
Bedford to Wellingborough D 31 9
Birmingham to Wolverhampton E253
Bletchley to Cambridge D 94 4
Bletchley to Rugby E 07 9
Bodmin - Branch Lines around B 83 1
Bournemouth to Evercreech Jn A 46 8
Bournemouth to Weymouth A 57 4
Bradshaw's Guide 1866 F 05 5
Bradshaw's History F18 5
Bradshaw's Rail Times 1850 F 13 0
Bradshaw's Rail Times 1895 F 11 6
Branch Lines series - see town names
Brecon to Neath D 43 2
Brecon to Newport D 16 6
Brecon to Newtown E 06 2
Brighton to Eastbourne A 16 1
Brighton to Worthing A 03 1
Bristol to Taunton D 03 6
Bromley South to Rochester B 23 7
Bromsgrove to Birmingham D 87 6
Bromsgrove to Gloucester D 73 9
Broxbourne to Cambridge F16 1
Brunel - A railtour D 74 6
Bude - Branch Line to B 29 9
Burnham to Evercreech Jn B 68 0

C
Cambridge to Ely D 55 5
Canterbury - BLs around B 58 9
Cardiff to Dowlais (Cae Harris) E 47 5
Cardiff to Pontypridd E 95 6
Cardiff to Swansea E 42 0
Carlisle to Hawick E 85 7
Carmarthen to Fishguard E 66 6
Caterham & Tattenham Corner B251
Central & Southern Spain NG E 91 8
Chard and Yeovil - BLs a C 30 7
Charing Cross to Dartford A 75 8
Charing Cross to Orpington A 96 3
Cheddar - Branch Line to B 90 9
Cheltenham to Andover C 43 7
Cheltenham to Redditch D 81 4
Chester to Birkenhead F 21 5
Chester to Rhyl E 93 2

Chichester to Portsmouth A 14 7
Clacton and Walton - BLs to F 04 8
Clapham Jn to Beckenham Jn B 36 7
Cleobury Mortimer - BLs a E 18 5
Clevedon & Portishead - BLs to D180
Consett to South Shields E 57 4
Cornwall Narrow Gauge D 56 2
Corris and Vale of Rheidol E 65 9
Craven Arms to Llandeilo E 35 2
Craven Arms to Wellington E 33 8
Crawley to Littlehampton A 34 5
Cromer - Branch Lines around C 26 0
Croydon to East Grinstead B 48 0
Crystal Palace & Catford Loop B 87 1
Cyprus Narrow Gauge E 13 0

D
Darjeeling Revisited F 09 3
Darlington Leamside Newcastle E 28 4
Darlington to Newcastle D 98 2
Dartford to Sittingbourne B 34 3
Derwent Valley - BL to the D 06 7
Devon Narrow Gauge E 09 3
Didcot to Banbury D 02 9
Didcot to Swindon C 84 0
Didcot to Winchester C 13 0
Dorset & Somerset NG D 76 0
Douglas - Laxey - Ramsey E 75 8
Douglas to Peel C 88 8
Douglas to Port Erin C 55 0
Douglas to Ramsey D 39 5
Dover to Ramsgate A 78 9
Dublin Northwards in 1950s E 31 4
Dunstable - Branch Lines to E 27 7

E
Ealing to Slough C 42 0
Eastbourne to Hastings A 27 7
East Cornwall Mineral Railways D 22 7
East Croydon to Three Bridges A 53 6
Eastern Spain Narrow Gauge E 56 7
East Grinstead - BLs to A 07 9
East London - Branch Lines of C 44 4
East London Line B 80 0
East of Norwich - Branch Lines E 69 7
Effingham Junction - BLs a A 74 1
Ely to Norwich C 90 1
Enfield Town & Palace Gates D 32 6
Epsom to Horsham A 30 7
Eritrean Narrow Gauge E 38 3
Euston to Harrow & Wealdstone C 89 5
Exeter to Barnstaple B 15 2
Exeter to Newton Abbot C 49 9
Exeter to Tavistock B 69 5
Exmouth - Branch Lines to B 00 8

F
Fairford - Branch Line to A 52 9
Falmouth, Helston & St. Ives C 74 1
Fareham to Salisbury A 67 3
Faversham to Dover B 05 3
Felixstowe & Aldeburgh - BL to D 20 3
Fenchurch Street to Barking C 20 8
Festiniog - 50 yrs of enterprise C 83 3
Festiniog 1946-55 E 01 7
Festiniog in the Fifties B 68 8
Festiniog in the Sixties B 91 6
Ffestiniog in Colour 1955-82 F 25 3
Finsbury Park to Alexandra Pal C 02 8
Frome to Bristol B 77 0

G
Gloucester to Bristol D 35 7
Gloucester to Cardiff D 66 1
Gosport - Branch Lines around A 36 9

Greece Narrow Gauge D 72 2

H
Hampshire Narrow Gauge D 36 4
Harrow to Watford D 14 2
Harwich & Hadleigh - BLs to F 02 4
Hastings to Ashford A 37 6
Hawkhurst - Branch Line to A 66 6
Hayling - Branch Line to A 12 3
Hay-on-Wye - BL around D 92 0
Haywards Heath to Seaford A 28 4
Hemel Hempstead - BLs to D 88 3
Henley, Windsor & Marlow - BLa C77 2
Hereford to Newport D 54 8
Hertford & Hatfield - BLs a E 58 1
Hertford Loop E 71 0
Hexham to Carlisle D 75 3
Hexham to Hawick F 08 6
Hitchin to Peterborough D 07 4
Holborn Viaduct to Lewisham A 81 9
Horsham - Branch Lines to A 02 4
Huntingdon - Branch Line to A 93 2

I
Ilford to Shenfield C 97 0
Ilfracombe - Branch Line to B 21 3
Industrial Rlys of the South East A 09 3
Ipswich to Saxmundham C 41 3
Isle of Wight Lines - 50 yrs C 12 3
Italy Narrow Gauge F 17 8

K
Kent Narrow Gauge C 45 1
Kidderminster to Shrewsbury E 10 9
Kingsbridge - Branch Line to C 98 7
Kings Cross to Potters Bar E 62 8
Kingston & Hounslow Loops A 83 3
Kingswear - Branch Line to C 17 8

L
Lambourn - Branch Line to C 70 3
Launceston & Princetown - BLs C 19 2
Lewisham to Dartford A 92 5
Lines around Wimbledon B 75 6
Liverpool Street to Chingford D 01 2
Liverpool Street to Ilford C 34 5
Llandeilo to Swansea E 46 8
London Bridge to Addiscombe B 20 6
London Bridge to East Croydon A 58 1
Longmoor - Branch Lines to A 41 3
Looe - Branch Line to C 22 2
Lowestoft - BLs around E 40 6
Ludlow to Hereford E 14 7
Lydney - Branch Lines around E 26 0
Lyme Regis - Branch Line to A 45 1
Lynton - Branch Line to B 04 6

M
Machynlleth to Barmouth E 54 3
Maesteg and Tondu Lines E 06 2
March - Branch Lines around B 09 1
Marylebone to Rickmansworth D 49 4
Melton Constable to Yarmouth Bch E031
Midhurst - Branch Lines of E 78 9
Midhurst - Branch Lines to F 00 0
Mitcham Junction Lines B 01 5
Mitchell & company C 59 8
Monmouth - Branch Lines to E 20 8
Monmouthshire Eastern Valleys D 71 5
Moretonhampstead - BL to C 27 7
Moreton-in-Marsh to Worcester D 26 5
Mountain Ash to Neath D 80 7

N
Newbury to Westbury C 66 6
Newcastle to Hexham D 69 2
Newport (IOW) - Branch Lines to A 26 0

Newquay - Branch Lines to C 71 0
Newton Abbot to Plymouth C 60 4
Newtown to Aberystwyth E 41 3
North East German NG D 44 9
Northern France Narrow Gauge C 75 8
Northern Spain Narrow Gauge E 83 3
North London Line B 94 7
North Woolwich - BLs around C 65 9

O
Ongar - Branch Line to E 05 5
Oswestry - Branch Lines around E 60 4
Oswestry to Whitchurch E 81 9
Oxford to Bletchley D 57 9
Oxford to Moreton-in-Marsh D 15 9

P
Paddington to Ealing C 37 6
Paddington to Princes Risborough C819
Padstow - Branch Line to B 54 1
Pembroke and Cardigan - BLs to F 29 1
Peterborough to Kings Lynn E 32 1
Plymouth - BLs around B 98 5
Plymouth to St. Austell C 63 5
Pontypool to Mountain Ash D 65 4
Pontypridd to Merthyr F 14 7
Pontypridd to Port Talbot E 84 4
Porthmadog 1954-94 - BLa B 31 2
Portmadoc 1923-46 - BLa B 13 8
Portsmouth to Southampton A 31 4
Portugal Narrow Gauge E 67 3
Potters Bar to Cambridge D 70 8
Princes Risborough - BL to D 05 0
Princes Risborough to Banbury C 85 7

R
Reading to Basingstoke B 27 5
Reading to Didcot C 79 6
Reading to Guildford A 47 5
Redhill to Ashford A 73 4
Return to Blaenau 1970-82 C 64 2
Rhyl to Bangor F 15 4
Rhymney & New Tredegar Lines E 48 2
Rickmansworth to Aylesbury D 61 6
Romania & Bulgaria NG E 23 9
Romneyrail C 32 1
Ross-on-Wye - BLs around E 30 7
Ruabon to Barmouth E 84 0
Rugby to Birmingham E 37 6
Rugby to Loughborough F 12 3
Rugby to Stafford F 07 9
Ryde to Ventnor A 19 2

S
Salisbury to Westbury B 39 8
Saxmundham to Yarmouth C 69 7
Saxony Narrow Gauge D 47 0
Seaton & Sidmouth - BLs to A 95 6
Selsey - Branch Line to A 04 8
Sheerness - Branch Line to B 16 2
Shenfield to Ipswich E 96 3
Shrewsbury - Branch Line to A 86 4
Shrewsbury to Chester E 70 3
Shrewsbury to Ludlow E 21 5
Shrewsbury to Newtown E 29 1
Sierra Leone Narrow Gauge D 28 9
Sirhowy Valley Line E 12 3
Sittingbourne to Ramsgate A 90 1
Slough to Newbury C 56 7
South African Two-foot gauge E 51 2
Southampton to Bournemouth A 42 0
Southend & Southminster BLs E 76 5
Southern Alpine Narrow Gauge F 22 2
Southern France Narrow Gauge C 47 5
South London Line B 46 6

South Lynn to Norwich City F
Southwold - Branch Line to A
Spalding - Branch Lines arou
St Albans to Bedford D 08 1
St. Austell to Penzance C 67
ST Isle of Wight A 56 7
Stourbridge to Wolverhampto
St. Pancras to Barking D 68 5
St. Pancras to Folkestone E 8
St. Pancras to St. Albans C 7
Stratford-u-Avon to Birmingh
Stratford-u-Avon to Cheltenh
ST West Hants A 69 7
Sudbury - Branch Lines to F
Surrey Narrow Gauge C 87 1
Sussex Narrow Gauge C 68
Swanley to Ashford B 45 9
Swansea to Carmarthen E 59
Swindon to Bristol C 96 3
Swindon to Gloucester D 46
Swindon to Newport D 30 2
Swiss Narrow Gauge C 94 9

T
Talyllyn 60 E 98 7
Taunton to Barnstaple B 60 2
Taunton to Exeter C 82 6
Tavistock to Plymouth B 88 6
Tenterden - Branch Line to A
Three Bridges to Brighton A 3
Tilbury Loop C 86 4
Tiverton - BLs around C 62 8
Tivetshall to Beccles D 41 8
Tonbridge to Hastings A 44 4
Torrington - Branch Lines to
Towcester - BLs around E 39
Tunbridge Wells BLs A 32 1

U
Upwell - Branch Line to B 64

V
Victoria to Bromley South A
Vivarais Revisited E 08 6

W
Wantage - Branch Line to D
Wareham to Swanage 50 yrs
Waterloo to Windsor A 54 3
Waterloo to Woking A 38 3
Watford to Leighton Buzzard
Welshpool to Llanfair E 49 9
Wenford Bridge to Fowey C
Westbury to Bath B 55 8
Westbury to Taunton C 76 5
West Cornwall Mineral Rlys
West Croydon to Epsom B 0
West German Narrow Gauge
West London - BLs of C 50 5
West London Line B 84 8
West London Line B 848
West Wiltshire - BLs of D 12
Weymouth - BLs A 65 9
Willesden Jn to Richmond B
Wimbledon to Beckenham C
Wimbledon to Epsom B 62 6
Wimborne - BLs around A 9
Wisbech - BLs around C 01
Witham & Kelvedon - BLs a
Woking to Alton A 59 8
Woking to Portsmouth A 25
Woking to Southampton A 5
Wolverhampton to Shrewsb
Worcester to Birmingham D
Worcester to Hereford D 38
Worthing to Chichester A 06
Wroxham - BLs around F 15

Y
Yeovil - 50 yrs change C 18
Yeovil to Dorchester A 76 5
Yeovil to Exeter A 91 8
York to Scarborough F 23 9